LIFE IS BUT A DREAM

A Memoir of Living with Illness

GARET SPIESE

STRATTON PRESS
We Celebrate Your Story

Life Is But A Dream
Copyright © 2022 **Garet Spiese**

Stratton Press Publishing
831 N Tatnall Street Suite M #188,
Wilmington, DE 19801
www.stratton-press.com
1-888-323-7009

ISBN (Paperback): 978-1-64895-793-2
ISBN (Ebook): 978-1-64895-794-9

Printed in the United States of America

For Stephen,
Without you I would not be in this world
Nor would I want to be.
You are my best of dreams
Forever

And in memory of
Shelton Morrison
Who will always be a part of me
And to whom I am forever
Grateful.

INTRODUCTION

We are living in unusual times. As I embark on this second release of *Life is but a Dream*, my heart aches with the grief for so many lost to Covid-19, those still suffering, and those family and friends affected by this demon. I hope that as you read this piece, you may find comfort and perhaps a few tools to help cope with the illness and the grief. Life is full of challenges, but also holds many wonders in each day. Let us hold tight to the light and look for all things good.

Journaling has been essential to my sanity and survival since my twelfth birthday when I was gifted a sky-blue diary. After reading Anne Frank's *Diary of a Young Girl*, I transitioned to lengthy entries in a school-paper notebook, where I could write longer entries. Those records, although no longer existent except in my memory, greatly informed the adolescent and teenage years documented here.

Since the inception of my illness, I have met with my various doctors at least once every three months. Each of them, in observing my determination and positive attitude, have commented repeatedly, "You should write a book." With each injury, esophageal bleed, infection, case of the flu, and the liver transplant itself, I apparently amazed doctors, nurses, and my family and friends by coming out on the other side with a smile. In 2004, three years following my liver transplant, I began documenting my journey in earnest. Many times since then, when I have been hospitalized for Lyme disease, heart problems, or bleed outs, I have prayed, "May I live just long enough to complete the book." I write this work to fulfill the admonition of my doctors, but more than that, I write for others who face uncertainty in illness or any other type of struggle.

I must admit, to write a book about oneself seems very self-indulgent. My story is indeed unique to me. However, each one of us struggles, learns, and grows through his or her own story. I am hoping that you can identify with some of my challenges and find hope and coping techniques by witnessing my journey.

Although centering upon my health experiences, this work is also a chronicle of my spiritual growth, from evangelical Christian to a step back from the faith to defining an individualized spirituality. I have come to believe that we are essentially eternal, enduring energy. This time we spend on earth, in this body, is an interlude in which we have the opportunity to learn, to grow, and to develop into a better version of ourselves. We are complex specimens of strength, wellness, love, and myriad other wonders. Therefore, the dream we call life unfolds with a profusion of unexpected turns.

There are many experiences, undocumented in this work, which have frightened, inspired, and molded me. A week and two days after the surgery, while I was still in the hospital, the nurses were instructed to wean me from supplemental oxygen. I felt as if I could not breathe without it, so I kept asking to be given the cannula. One kind nurse told me firmly, "God made you so that you can breathe. You must trust your body to do what it knows you need." I thought of a song to encourage me. So I sang, "Down from his glory…my God and Savior came…my breath, my sunshine, my all in all…" Just by singing, I exercised my lungs, and could breathe more easily.

The hospital room was temperature-controlled. At home, I was challenged to breathe normal May-temperature air. When I was discharged from Johns Hopkins, my first evening at home was a nightmare. As darkness fell, I felt like the atmosphere was pressing in upon me. I could not take breaths deep enough to sustain me. The more I gasped for breath, the more frightened I became. I was so distraught, Steve phoned Johns Hopkins to speak with our assigned physician's assistant. She spoke with me directly, coaching me through this panic attack. As I breathed deeply and slowly, the world became a friendlier place for me. I found I could, indeed, breathe on my own. All was well.

Within the year following transplant, my body began rejecting the new liver. Another hospitalization at Johns Hopkins was filled with pain and uncertainty. A duct between the donated liver and my own intestinal tract was scarring shut. With the placement of a stent, the problem resolved. For a while, we were uncertain if my body would accept its gift. Dr. Luis Arrazola assured my mother, "Showers will come, but the storm is over."

So yes, showers continue to occur from time to time.

In 2002, following a silly misstep during a play rehearsal, I aggravated a hitherto undetected condition of vascular necrosis. In short, years of prednisone had resulted in the destruction of the meniscus in my knee, so within a few months, I was limping bone-on-bone. In July 2003, under the skilled hands of Dr. Khanujah at Johns Hopkins, I received a total replacement of the right knee.

Since 1999, when doctors prescribed insulin to more tightly control blood sugar levels, Steve has rescued me from multiple episodes of hypoglycemia (low blood sugar). Once, he came home after teaching a music lesson, to find me unconscious on the kitchen floor. My memory of this incident is coming to, while sitting on the living room couch, Steve stuffing peanut butter crackers and pouring orange juice into my mouth.

In each of these instances, I somehow pulled through. Prayer, love, and gratitude were effectual in my recoveries. Looking back on all this, the flow of my life seems truly dream-like.

I hope by reading this work, no matter what your situation, you find inspiration to persevere, to take care of the illness or problem, but to focus on living. I have found great strength and peace in being grateful for each day. I hope, also, that those who are in the medical profession may gain insight into the experience of the patient. My gratitude cannot be fully expressed for the excellent care I have received from these extraordinary people.

Elements of my survival include:
- Positive attitude instilled in me by my parents' own example
- Faith and hope that tomorrow will be a better day
- The expert vigilance of those in medicine

- Gratitude for each new day
- An inspiring and devoted life partner

Not one of us, whether healthy or ailing, knows what a day may bring or if we will see tomorrow. It is best to experience to the fullest whatever comes to us today. We will be better persons for it when tomorrow comes. After all, life is but a dream.

ACKNOWLEDGMENTS

My life has been a dream.

In the making of it all, I must thank my wonderful friends and family.

My brother, Rich, introduced me to theater and acting. He taught me so much about being aware of others, being alert to my own surroundings and space (this is important when you must be careful of bumping into things!), and taking the chance to try.

My brother, Tim, helped me to be able, once again, to walk through the woods with enough sense to see that briars and twigs can be avoided, moved, or stepped upon, so that you don't come home all bloodied up. He gave me the freedom to enjoy camping and the out-of-doors, my dear Mother Earth. I am forever grateful to him for this.

My sister, Kathy, dropped everything she was doing so she could take me to the hospital when I called to say I was in trouble due to bleeding. While waiting for transplant, I told her I needed to ask the Johns Hopkins social worker what kind of care I might need following transplant and for how long, so I could arrange caregivers to come to my home. Kathy answered, "Oh, didn't I tell you? When I was hired at the day-care center, I told them I would be leaving as soon as my sister had her transplant. I'm going to take care of you."

My precious husband, Steve, has taught me that anything is possible. *I can't* is not part of his vocabulary. Steve has entertained me since the first day I met him—acting, making jokes, playing his guitar and trumpet, composing at the piano, singing, and generally having fun. He has been my primary caregiver through countless injuries and illnesses. I would not be on this earth if not for his vigilance and advocacy.

My dearest mother, Treva, who was my greatest advocate and caregiver before Steve came into our lives. She could never do enough to satisfy her desire to cook nutritious foods, to provide us with household necessities, and to provide money to cover unexpected expenses. Her love knew no bounds.

My wonderful father, Glenn, who always helped me see the good in whatever experience came along. When I was dealing with my leg wound, I cried, "Oh, Daddy. I know they won't let me get a transplant before this wound is healed. And how long might that be?" But he stroked my back. "Just think of all the things doctors will learn in the meantime. Every day, they are making more and more amazing advances. This just gives them a little more time before it's your turn." He has forever helped me see that there is hope for tomorrow.

Then there is Alice, who I met one summer while working at River Valley Ranch, the Bob Jones University of summer camps. Alice had traveled to Indiana to visit relatives, to Sweden to visit relatives, and who knows where else? She lived in Silver Spring, Maryland, and spent a lot of time in Washington, DC. She was so kind to me. Alice is an artist, very gregarious, and very likeable. Her list of friends would fill a library; her overseas trips as missionary and tourist, several books. I feel so blessed to be among those friends. Fortunately, we have kept in touch over the years, mostly due to her efforts. She remains one of my dearest friends and supporters.

Those invaluable friends, who, by serving with our fundraising organization, *Garet's Hope,* have given of themselves freely to provide moral support and financial resources.

Expert healthcare providers, without whom I would not be writing this today:

Dr. Roebling Knoch and Dr. Frank McKeon of York Hospital, York, Pennsylvania

Dr. William B. Thorsen and Dr. James Srour, gastroenterologists, York, Pennsylvania

Dr. Anna Mae Diehl, liver transplant evaluator, Johns Hopkins Medical Center, Baltimore, Maryland

Dr. Ayesha Jafri, Lancaster General Health System, Columbia-Wrightsville, Pennsylvania

Dr. Shefali M. Shah, Lancaster General Health System, Wrightsville, Pennsylvania

Drs. James Burdick and Robert Montgomery, transplant surgeons, Johns Hopkins

Dr. Michael Flood, wound healer extraordinaire, Lancaster, Pennsylvania

Dr. Luis Arrazola, hepatologist, Johns Hopkins

Dr. Paul Thuluvath, hepatologist, Johns Hopkins, now at Mercy Medical Center

And so many more…

Nurses who have comforted;

Friends who have supported and encouraged, especially Suanne who took the time to read an early manuscript and give valuable suggestions;

Denise Benefiel, of iUniverse, who urged me to initially publish my story;

Dr. Arthur Ford, my former English professor at Lebanon Valley College, who praised and coached me and gave me the confidence to make this publication a reality; and more LVC English professors, Dr. John Kearney and Dr. Phil Billings, who gave me many opportunities to be creative.

Family who have loved and motivated and cared for me, listened to my complaints, and cleaned up my messes.

And very importantly, My Organ Donor, for her selfless decision to, upon her death, save other lives, including mine.

My deepest gratitude to these and numberless others unnamed here, strangers and acquaintances, who have passed through my life and left their mark on my dream.

AUTHOR'S NOTE

Throughout this work, I have presented the story using dreams, journal entries, and narrative. Dreams are generally presented *in italics*. Journal entries are dated and *in italics*. The narrative regarding my adolescence and my initial diagnosis was written largely from memories, plus a bit of creative license. Since I destroyed my first and most revealing journal, *Kim*, I had to recreate these entries. This was not a difficult task since I had pretty much seared them into my mind, reading and rereading them until I was seventeen. Other journal entries, although slightly modified in some cases, are lifted from existing journals, written to help get me through further medical challenges.

The very fact that I have reached my sixty-fifth birthday is a dream. Looking back over the many frightening experiences I have gone through, accompanied by extremely satisfying, joyful events, my sense of it all is withdrawn, as if someone else lived that life. Or I lived it in a dream. For this reason, I felt the necessity to include dreams, sometimes as foreshadowing of an incident in my life, sometimes simply to reveal my state of mind.

I trust my audience will be able to discern my motives and the infrastructure of this piece.

Row, row, row your boat
Gently down the stream.
Merrily, merrily, merrily, merrily,
Life is but a dream.

A DREAM

No luck. Won't budge. I throw my weight into my hip and turn the knob with my hand. Push with all my might. Still, the door won't open. I grope through the cold, dark corridor along the wall until I feel the frame of another door. Again, I find the knob, turn, and push. Again, nothing but resistance. Onward I advance through this pitch-black world. Why is there no light?

Why won't these doors give? Another door frame under my touch as I inch along. "Please, open this time." I cannot get enough breath. I grasp the knob, take a deep breath, and place my shoulder and hip against the door. Push. Push again. Each door seems full of possibility as I anticipate its opening into whatever it is I seek. Full of hope, I thrust myself against the next door, but the door will not budge. What is forbidden to me to see? To experience? Even beyond just one?

I choke back tears as the door remains solid. Something inside compels me to move ahead. Just one more try. My throat feels tight. This darkness is smothering. Ah! Another door frame. Smooth varnish under my fingertips, with simple intricate levels carved in, like the doors in my own house. Surely, this one will let me through, release me from the dark world I fear.

Slowly, now. Don't rush it. I grasp the knob. Turn it. And push. I press against the door with my whole body. Push. No success. No give. My cheek against the wood, I release my hand and slide to the floor, sobbing. I'm so tired. I just want to give up. How long must this go on?

Carefully, I hoist myself upright and resume my blind trek down the hallway. Suddenly, in the distance, there appears a square of gray (I am *afraid to guess) light in the middle of this smothering sheath of darkest night. An option in the impenetrable density of certain prohibition. An escape from perpetual darkness. An opportunity to be free from this everlasting night?*

Measuring each step, I approach, almost not breathing for fear it will disappear. The square grows larger with each step until, there I am, standing just before it. The gray seems a thick fog. I cannot see what is in it. Could I step through this window and fall? Could I step through and find—what? As in darkness, there is no real definition in the haze either. At least in the blackness I am pushing, struggling against something. I know what darkness is about. Yet although there lies uncertainty in the mist, there also exists the allure of possibility.

I step through the window with a sense of hope, and then...
I awaken.

CHAPTER 1

A Life-Changing Possibility

My stomach instantly swims with wiggling crawlers. A hole seems to open in my throat, and for a moment, I cannot breathe. The clinical voice is muffled as blood pounds in my ears.

"It is imperative that you be placed on the liver transplant list. You have entered what we call end-stage liver disease."

This has to be a dream. Any moment I will awaken under the warm comforter beside my husband, Steve, with my cat purring on the bed.

"Your enzyme levels remain steady but extremely elevated," the salt-and-pepper-haired young doctor navigates the top pages of my three-inch thick file. "As you know, you have survived the hepatitis far longer than we ever could have anticipated. But now your liver is becoming less and less functional." He places a gentle hand on my shoulder. "I guess we could say it's tired and worn out."

This is nearly impossible for me to believe, even though it is scientifically rational. After all, the first diagnosis of a rare liver disorder came thirty-eight years ago when I was a thirteen-year-old active adolescent. Since then, the disease has been controlled with medication and guarded vigilantly with blood tests and doctor visits every three months. Periodic hospitalizations and hazards of internal bleeding and easy laceration have interrupted my determined attempts at normal activity. But in spite of everything, I have survived.

It took twenty years before my doctors named my disorder. Autoimmune hepatitis had, along with other autoimmune diseases, remained a mystery to the medical community until we became aware of AIDS in the United States in the early 1980s. (The acronym AIDS was suggested at a meeting in Washington, DC, in July 1982: http://www.avert.org/aids-history-86.htm).

Autoimmune deficiency syndrome, or AIDS, is the body's inability to fight off disease because of an underactive or inactive immune system. On the opposite end of the scale, there are cases in which the immune system malfunctions by overreacting. In these automatic immune responses, the immune system notes a slight abnormality, like a leftover pox mark, in a healthy part of the body, as diseased and attacks it. The attack could be caused by an imprint left by a virus from which the person has already recovered. The number of other variables which may cause autoimmune disease is myriad.

Autoimmune hepatitis, I was soon to learn, strikes one in ten thousand, usually women aged twenty-five to forty. It turns out, I was that one, an exception as I was only an adolescent when I first became seriously ill.

Through my thundering heartbeat, I barely hear Doctor Srour continue. "You could have the transplant in Philadelphia, Pittsburgh, or Baltimore. Which would you prefer?"

A liver transplant. This is beyond my scope of comprehension. I had read of great advancements in medicine. I remember hearing the news of Dr. Christiaan Barnard's successful heart transplant in South Africa in 1967. It is indeed wonderful that, today, lives that previously may have been cut short can be prolonged through the miracles of medical procedure. But I never considered myself as part of that grand picture.

As the sterile walls of the doctor's office glare upon me, I puzzle, Is this for me? Haven't I already lived thirty-five years beyond the expected fourteen days when I was first hospitalized? In my forty-seven years, I've helped nurture three nephews and five nieces. I am godmother to three lovely little girls now grown into young women. I've written and performed a one-woman consciousness-raising play. I have created and presented original stories as a storyteller. I've had the privilege of adapting for the stage a book of poetry by one of my own college professors. Presently, I am living my life as any normal, healthy person would, with a few exceptions. True, I begin each morning with a handful of pills and pop others routinely throughout the day. I have to be careful at my part-time job at the theater not to bump into the copier or desk or scattered Rubbermaid crates of props and costumes for fear of easy bruising, hematoma, or laceration which may require a trip to the hospital. When I return home in the evening, I need to elevate my legs to relieve some of the swelling caused not only by my poor vascular uptake, but also because of continued ingestion of the drug, prednisone.

But I have focused on living, jamming into whatever time I have left, activities that I love—acting, writing, storytelling, volunteering—the liver disorder has taken a place on the back burner of my consciousness. My life is busier and fuller than the lives of many of my closest friends and associates who are vitally healthy.

"What more is there left for me to do?" I wonder. "What more can I ask of life?"

"Peggy? Did you hear me?" persists the distant voice of Dr. Srour. "I'd like to set you up with an appointment before you leave today."

Do I have a choice in this? Shouldn't I take time to think about it? An organ transplant is a huge step. A life-changing option. I feel as though I am stepping into a world of misty uncertainty.

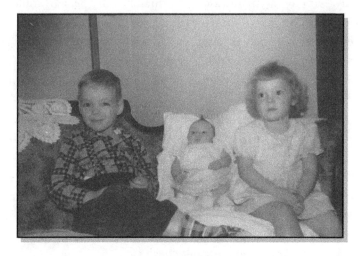

Richard, Kathy, Peggy
Christmas 1952

Glenn, Treva, Timmy, Richard, Kathy, Peggy
Christmas 1960

CHAPTER 2

The Onset

Until I was forty-seven years old, whenever I heard the word *transplant*, it meant to me that my African violet had grown too big for its pot, so it needed to be moved to a larger planter. Then, in the last few years as I worked for a small theater, a character named Morgan Donor emerged from an improvisational comedy group there. In the sketch, a bearded fellow wearing dark glasses and a beret entered stage-right, introducing himself as Morgan Donor. He described himself as "a poet with real heart, a true liver of life, a recent transplant from Lung Island," and as the audience howled with laughter, he exclaimed, "No kidney!"

Ironically, these light associations with the word *transplant* soon took on a life or death significance for me. In December 1997, during this routine six-month visit with my gastroenterologist, he concluded it was time for me to be placed on a transplant list. My liver had far outlasted its longevity and usefulness. It could fail me suddenly, at any time.

I felt fine, all things considered. I had learned to live with a subnormal functioning body. Due to years of taking prednisone, my tissues had lost their resiliency. A tiny bump into the corner of a desk could result in a severe laceration requiring stitches. The prednisone had also caused diabetes, which was discovered when I was about thirty-five years old. I was placed on oral medication to control the glucose levels. Additionally, I was developing cataracts, due to prolonged steroid treatment. In contrast to those of my friends and colleagues, my life was strictly regimented. To prevent potential accidents, I practiced heightened awareness. Taking medicine every day, being extra careful, and dealing with an accident should one occur was routine. In spite of it all, I was still alive and walking around!

I was twelve years old when this adventure began.

Most of us remember 1963 for Dr. Martin Luther King's historic speech, "I Have a Dream" on the steps of the Lincoln Memorial, the Los Angeles Dodgers' World Series victory over the New York Yankees, and the most impactful event, the assassination of John Fitzgerald Kennedy. As a pre-teenage girl, I was immersed in school activities: student government, chorus, and cheerleading. I had a huge crush on a boy in my church youth group and, in my circle of friends, girls spent all their time talking about boys and how to dress to attract boys, what might happen at the dance or skating party or other group events where girls could meet with boys.

The biggest physical problems female adolescents had to deal with were occasional acne and the dreaded *period*.

However, for me, little troubles began to interfere with this joyful continuum. When my menstrual period failed to come at its usual time in February 1963, I was overjoyed. It had been a nuisance since it came upon me at ten years of age. It had interrupted swimming plans and sleepover dates. So when it didn't show up in February and then again in March, I was quite content. At age twelve, I didn't think at all about how unnatural this cessation was. I never reported it to my mother, who, I later learned, was well aware that it had stopped.

I was also plagued by occasional breakouts of pimples on my face. This was not particularly remarkable for girls my age. However, my mother had never had to deal with skin problems and so she was suspicious of my blood chemistry.

I hardly allowed these abnormalities to interfere with my happily busy routine. When the announcement came over the loudspeaker one day in school that I had been chosen as a junior high cheerleader, I was overjoyed. It was so exciting to do the routines with the other girls. It put me in the popular group. I was good at it, and it gave me confidence. I had lots of contagious enthusiasm and my love for dancing helped me to execute the choreographed routines.

But as a cheerleader, I was expected to have good energy and extra stamina. Imagine my disappointment when, only a few months after I was chosen, my energy began to wane. A good friend prodded me, "Cheerleaders are supposed to be peppy, Peggy. What's the matter with you?"

After practicing just a few cheers, I was exhausted. The cheering routines often involved clapping hands and slapping hands on the thighs in rhythm. After cheerleading practice, my thighs were not just red but mottled purple from the slapping. Unknowingly, I was bruising myself and breaking blood vessels.

At age twelve, I, like most other adolescents, was anxious for acceptance by my peers and very conscious of my appearance. One evening at choir practice, I sat next to my fair-skinned friend, Janna. I, too, was fair complected, and with summer approaching, we both wanted to have tanned skin. So that evening, during soprano and tenor part drills (we were altos), Janna and I compared the hue of our inner arms. Janna's was a smooth pale pink. Mine was a smooth sallow yellow. Since I was darker, I thought I was more tan than Janna. Actually, I learned later, my skin was yellow because my blood was retaining toxic levels of bilirubin.

At school, my friend Carolyn and I began a weight-losing competition. Both of us were approximately five feet, two inches tall. I weighed in at 112 pounds, Carolyn weighed 115 pounds. We decided we each needed to lose ten pounds. Then we measured our waists. One of my very favorite skirts was a rainbow plaid A-line with attached suspender-type straps. It had a broader than usual waistband, about four and a half inches, that fit my twenty-four-inch waist perfectly. Of all the hand-me-downs I had received from my cousin Bev, this was my all-time favorite. Soon, I hoped, it would fit a little more loosely. Carolyn and I met each other in second grade at age seven. We were always the tallest girls in our class and reached our then current height by age eleven. We were not fat, but being taller made us feel like we were larger than we should be.

Just a few weeks after we best friends made our weight and inches losing pact, I came home from school doubled over with pain. Hoping to gain some relief, I threw my books on the dining room table, loosened my skirt, and fell onto the sofa. Nothing eased the extreme piercing in my abdomen.

I lay writhing on the couch. But when my mother proclaimed, "Well, you're not going to church meeting this evening," I protested, "I have to! I'm supposed to read the scripture!"

Little did I know it, but the lessons of living with illness were just beginning. If I couldn't be in church to read the scripture, someone else would read it instead. I was not indispensable.

CHAPTER 3

Non-Judgmental Friend

November 12, 1963

Dear Kim,

Since I just finished reading The Diary of Anne Frank, I decided to make my own diary with notebook paper. She called her diary Kitty. I decided to name mine Kim. It will be like writing letters to my best friend. I like this much better than the little blue leather-covered diary with a lock and key. I got it as a present for my twelfth birthday. But it only has five little lines for each day. By writing letters to you in this notebook, Kim, I can write as much as I want.

Today went okay. I only saw Richard F. one time in the hall at school right before English. He is so cute! The Youth Fellowship Group has set a date for the roller-skating party. Can't wait. I'm sure Richard will ask me to skate at least once. I love skating!

Well, tomorrow is a geography quiz. Wonder what stupid questions Mr. Humme will have on this one. Like,

"How many cows are in the photo on page 47?" Guess I better study a little bit anyway.
    I'll be back tomorrow.

Love,
Peggy

Kathy, Treva, Peggy
Spring 1962

Cheerleader, Winter 1963

November 17, 1963

Dear Kim,

Sorry it's been so long since I've written to you. (Or should that be, in you?)

I've just been so tired lately. Maybe I'm just lazy. I think that's what Mother thinks. I dry a few dishes and feel like I have to sit for five minutes. Then she gets all upset with me.

I just want to stay in my room all day. But I have to sweep the front porch and steps at least. I should also practice my stupid voice lesson. I wish Mrs. Shepherd would give me a piece I like. Sometimes, I think I don't even want to take lessons anymore. I sure don't want to end up singing like an opera singer!

Brother Richie says I do a good Connie Frances. That's the kind of song I like, "Lipstick on Your Collar,

Told a Tale on You." And sometimes, I think I'm never going to make it up that hill to voice lessons. Why does my teacher have to live at the very top of Church Street?

Sorry, Kim. I'm really complaining today. But at least you listen.

Only six more days until the skating party.

I'll see Richard F. tomorrow morning in church. It's okay. But you know, parents are there and brothers and sisters. And besides all that, Janna flirts with him. I don't know who he likes best, Janna or me.

I'll try to write sooner next time.

Love,
Peggy

November 22, 1963

Dear Kim,

The most awful thing has happened. President Kennedy was shot and killed this afternoon. I was sitting in the cafeteria in study hall working on algebra problems. Then Mr. Krebs announced over the loudspeaker, "President Kennedy has been shot in Dallas, Texas. His condition is not yet known."

It was like the wind was knocked out of me. Like someone had punched me in the stomach, and I couldn't breathe right.

Right away, I started silently praying for him. Vivian Shearer walked over to me and asked to borrow my Bible. I always carry my Bible to school—I learned at YFC (Youth for Christ) in a movie there that if you carry your Bible in school, it's a good testimony. Also, if an opportunity opens up, you might be able to lead someone to Christ.

I was glad I had it today. Vivian had hardly gotten back to her seat when we heard the loudspeaker crackle again.

"I'm sorry to announce that the president has died."

It sounded like Mr. Krebs was almost crying. Mrs. Newell, the study hall teacher, pulled a packet of Kleenex from her briefcase. Everyone was very quiet.

I don't know if we'll have school tomorrow or not. Tomorrow's skating party has been cancelled. I can't believe it. I was looking forward to it for so long! They're canceling everything—meetings, football games. And I just got my cheerleading uniform cleaned!

I don't get it. Must the whole world stop because of this?

Love,
Peggy

CHAPTER 4

Strange Symptoms

Days passed. I talked with my girlfriends about boyfriends. I played games and watched TV with my four-year-old brother, Tim, and ten-year-old sister, Kathy. I witnessed my big brother, Richard, celebrate his sixteenth birthday and earn his driver's license.

As I sat in one of the orange vinyl chairs in my mother's third floor beauty shop, I watched as the popular guys and girls, who were Richard's friends in the junior class, arrived to celebrate his sixteenth birthday Earlier that day, Mother had allowed his friends to decorate the shop with tissue paper flowers and red and white streamers and a big Happy Birthday banner hung across the dressing table mirror for the surprise birthday party. Other fifteen- to seventeen-year-olds filled the room before Richard finally arrived as they screamed, "Surprise!" They laughed and played music and fooled around with the equipment in the shop—the washing sink and the hairdryers. With little energy and no desire to participate in the fun, I felt poorly and extremely out of place.

That was February 17, 1963, and by that time, I had begun to feel very badly most of the time. As a sense of nausea overcame me and an intense pressure welled up in my stomach, I found that the only way to relieve this was with a belch, a silent release of air pressure through my mouth. But the taste and smell of it was sulphurous, like flatulence.

So every time one of these *mouth farts* occurred, I attempted to blow it away by puffing all the foul air out of my body. "Puh-puh-puh." I always had a ready supply of mints or mint gum. At age twelve, I was concerned only with being accepted by the popular kids at school. Health considerations were the farthest thing from my mind.

Then, one Sunday morning, my entire family attended church as usual. Once again, I had spent the hours in church and Sunday school pretending that I felt just fine. However, afterward, as the car pulled into the driveway, before Daddy had even shut off the engine, I leapt from the car, dashed across the footbridge, up the steps and into the kitchen. I barely made it to the kitchen sink in time to lean over and vomit.

Mother scolded me, "Why didn't you throw up outside somewhere where the rain could wash it away? Now I have to clean that up!" But later, she said it was a good thing I expelled the stuff into the sink because, that way, she could see what had come out of my body.

It frightened her. It frightened me. I knew it seemed like something that should have been expelled from my rectum. Just like the mouth farts.

All I knew was that I felt bad.

My mother was a lovely simple woman who grew up on a farm. She was also quite intelligent. She had noticed that I wasn't having my menstrual cycle. The obvious evidence was not appearing in the bathroom trashcan. She also knew that I never missed school unless I was feeling very sick, and I was missing a lot lately. Mother had noted that usually minor scratches from a paper cut or torn skin from a hangnail on her daughter had recently become lingering infections.

So in early January 1964, she once again took me to the doctor. She had taken me, her second child, to be examined by him several times before for these abnormalities, but he told her there was nothing wrong with me. He explained my yellow complexion by asserting that she was feeding me too much vitamin A.

"Keep her off carrots for a while, and the color will go away."

His remedy for the ceased menstrual cycle was a hormone shot. To this day, no one knows for sure what was in that injection. By now, fifty-plus years later, most likely, the records have been destroyed. However, in the years following the hormone injection, every time another doctor learned of this treatment, each of them echoed one message: "Never give a hormone injection to a child in adolescence."

Ultimately, it was Mother who saved me. Drawing on her home-remedied upbringing, she asked the doctor, "Isn't there a spring tonic that can clean this child's blood?"

Overall, the entire family had always been very healthy, both parents and four children. Mother cooked and served healthy balanced meals. As little ones, the children had received all the required inoculations and were given vitamin supplements.

When we came down with a cold, Mother gave us a Bayer children's aspirin. If we had an upset stomach or sore throat, the treatment was hot tea and toast. A fever required bed rest, aspirin, and Jell-O or popsicles.

Each of us children occasionally complained of an earache. There was a swimming pool on our country property, and we loved the water. The pool, essentially just a cemented pond, was fed by a stream which flowed in front of the house. At one end of the pool, a pipe poured in water from the dam in the creek upstream. At the other end, there was an overflow trough. So the water was constantly running in and flowing out. The temperature of the pool was spring water cold. Perhaps it was the water temperature, perhaps the fact that the water wasn't filtered or treated, or perhaps because we were in the pool a minimum of two hours every day in the summer that we suffered many earaches and ear infections as children.

However, these were the most serious ailments the family ever had—cold, sore throat, brief fever, and an occasional earache.

So it was with great restraint that Mother, instead of saying to the doctor, "There is obviously something very wrong with this kid's blood. You are a doctor. Can't you help her?" she calmly asked for a spring tonic to clean my blood.

With a patronizing smile, the doctor answered, "Well, no. But we could have her blood tested."

So at last, he wrote an order for blood work.

Treva at the Country Home
Fall 1955

CHAPTER 5

Knowledge Is Power

Mother was a beautician. Although she was busy raising a family of four children, she always made time to fit friends and neighbors into her schedule if they needed a haircut or wash and set. Besides her regular appointments in the beauty shop on Thursday and Friday, she went into ladies' homes when they couldn't get to the shop because of illness or frailty.

On an unusually warm day in late January, Mother placed a kitchen chair onto the back porch. Our next-door neighbor, Ginny, sat perched on the chair draped with a pink plastic cape which Mother used to protect her customer's clothing from falling clipped hair. I sat on the steps to the porch, watching, as Ginny sat very still and Mother deftly cut her hair. I was always fascinated with the ease of Mother's fingers as she held a small lock of hair between the first and second fingers of her left hand and snip-snipped with the scissors in her right hand. I also enjoyed just being nearby to hear Ginny tell stories of everyday events on her farm down the road or at her job in town. She always saw the funny side of things, the good part.

That particular day, the topic of conversation turned to me and my health. After the haircut, Mother was going to take me to the nearby city of York for the blood test. As Mother snipped, Ginny sat very still, except for her lips as she spoke. Not true. Her honest gray eyes were animated with great concern.

"A blood test is good. If there's nothing wrong, you'll find out. Or maybe it's something that can be fixed with a little medicine. At least, this way, you will know and not have to keep wondering."

Ginny was always so practical. If there was a problem, there had to be a solution. That day on the porch steps, listening to Ginny's confident statement, became a vivid memory. A warm sense of security washed over me. It lasted only a moment, but it was a moment I would visit again and again over the years. Although I was very frightened of what lay ahead, in my heart, I was certain that Ginny was right.

What that thirteen-year-old cheerleader did not know was how terrible the news would be and how long it would take to "fix it."

Feb. 28, 1964

Dear Kim,

I have to hurry. The blood testing lab, Dr. Paul's, closes at 8:00 and it's 6:15 now. Can you believe it? Mother phoned Dr. Robinson to ask what the results were from my blood test taken back in January, and he said he never got any report. But he never called to ask where it was! So now, I have to go back and get stuck again. It's so scary. I hate it. I wish I felt better—most of the time, I feel like throwing up. And then it goes away.

Kathy is going to stay overnight at Cindy's tonight and then tomorrow, Aunt Mary Ellen is taking them shopping. I wish I could go sledding over at Flemmens' house. But Mother says she wants me here at home. I guess I'll work on my short story and clean our room.

It's time to leave. Boo-hoo. Wish me luck.

Love,
Peggy

A DREAM

M y family is gathered with me in the kitchen. Mother and Daddy, younger sister Kathy, big brother Richard, and little Timmy are casually standing or sitting, each in their own little space. Kathy plays with her stuffed kitten near the stove in the corner. Richard sits at the table, his face in a book, studying chess moves with his game board and pieces before him. Timmy steps from one tile to another absorbed in his own imagination. Mother and Daddy move subtly from one area to another, but I don't know exactly what they are doing. We feel safe and comfortable here together in this familiar place, until—

Tramp. Tramp. Tramp. I hear them crunching and crashing through the woods which are our "backyard" hill. As I am paralyzed with fear, no one else seems to notice the unusual disturbance in our normally quiet surroundings.

Cautiously, I peer out the window of the old oak back door. Soldiers. Men dressed in drab green, wearing non-descript helmets, and toting big firearms. Slashing, smashing, heedlessly destroying our long-time leafy playground.

My anxiety mounts as they charge onto our back porch. Somehow, I know that they are coming to take my precious little brother from us. No word has been spoken to that effect, but the terror that grips my heart tells me it is so.

Mother and Daddy greet these men like neighbors. They are always kind to strangers. As a few of the soldiers barge into our kitchen, my brothers and sister take no notice.

Without explanation, two soldiers grab Tim, one at each arm. He does not resist their pull which will take him from all that is warm and friendly. He is totally passive and shows no fear or despair.

With all my might, I scream, "Daddy! Mother! Stop them! We don't have to do as they say! Do something! They have Timmy!"

My heart is breaking. I want to kick and beat these men out of our peaceful home. But I am helpless to make a difference. Everyone else in the household acts as if all is well. We must resign ourselves to this event, however disturbing it may be.

Heartbroken and weeping,
I awaken.

CHAPTER 6

Life Interrupted

On Wednesday, March 4, 1964, I sit in eighth-grade geography class doodling in a worn, red paper-covered notebook. Would Mr. Hamme ever say anything interesting? What does it matter how much rain falls in Brazil every year? Then, suddenly, an announcement comes over the loudspeaker: "Peggy Whorl, please report to the office immediately."

The chain of interesting events is just beginning.

Within the hour, I am whisked away in my mother's '59 Chevy. In the car, Mother explains, "Dr. Knoch called and said your blood tests show that you are a very sick girl. He wants you to be admitted to the hospital for a few days."

But what am I to do about cheerleading practice and the game this Saturday and youth group and choir practice?

On this gray March day in downtown York, one-way Market Street buzzes as usual with two lanes of cars whizzing by. A lady walks down the sidewalk splashing through muddy puddles, a bundled-up toddler by her side.

I sit alone in the car, watching little rivers as they rush into sewer drains. A young woman in a crisp fitted suit hurries across the street from the opposite side. She fumbles to unlock the door of the car parked directly in front of the one in which I wait. The lady juggles her brief-case to the passenger seat and climbs in behind the wheel. I wonder if this young woman has just closed a deal and is on her way to another meeting. Routine day-to-day activities for everyday people.

I turn my gaze to my right, to the storefront window with big red let-ters arched across the glass: *MORAMARCO'S BUSINESS MACHINES.* Daddy comes here to fix typewriters and adding machines five days a week, all but two weeks a year, and has been doing so for a long, long time. Computers do not yet belong to the common man. They are con-fined to huge research centers and the space program.

Mother has stopped here to tell Daddy face to face about the doc-tor's urgent orders to get me to the hospital. Right now, I have no idea what is transpiring between the thirty-nine-year-old couple in their hour of crisis inside this old brick building.

Up to this time, their lives have been challenging but livable, rel-atively normal. City born and raised Glenn and farm raised Treva (pro-nounced *Tree-vuh*) were married twenty years before at age twenty. In 1944, Treva took a brief vacation from her job as beautician at Bear's Department Store, borrowed her sister's wedding dress, packed a small suitcase, and traveled alone to Del Ray Beach, Florida, to marry Glenn, a private first-class in the Army Air Force. His tour of duty allowed him a couple of weeks' leave, but then back to the service for another two years. His commission took him from Fort Lauderdale, to Wisconsin, to California, and back before the happy young couple could set up housekeeping in Freysville. Glenn went to work repairing typewriters for a Remington dealer and Treva continued her profession in hairdress-ing. Between their favorite activities—roller skating, gardening, hunt-ing, and playing cards with friends—the attractive, happy newlyweds started a family.

Shortly after their first child Richard was born, they took a small loan from Glenn's uncle and purchased a three-bedroom home with a backyard. They chose this lovely little white-sided house on a tree-lined street because, with a beauty salon attached to it, Treva could take care of her toddler and still continue to work full-time. In the twenty-first century, it is common for a woman to juggle a career, marriage, house-keeping, and motherhood. In 1949, Treva was way ahead of her time.

It never occurred to Glenn that, in addition to working full-time, he should do anything but help with the family every way he could. He did his part of the housekeeping, cooking, and childcare. Treva loved hairdressing, and she enjoyed being a mother and wife. Glenn helped with the children and did his best to make a happy family.

He certainly succeeded in that. In 1950, the second child was born, Margaret Ann, named after Glenn's only sister, and nicknamed Peggy. Two years later on the very same day, August 31, another beautiful, precious little girl, Kathryn Sue, joined the healthy family.

By 1955, Glenn and Treva decided they would like to raise their children in the country, cultivating in them a love of trees, wildlife, and unpopulated space. The opportunity to purchase a little home on seven and a half acres in the lush wooded hollows outside of Glen Rock presented itself. After five years in this idyllic setting, a fourth healthy child was born, Timothy Brian.

This average American family led normal lives, attending the nearby sixty-eight-member country church, working, growing a vegetable garden, entertaining guests, and enjoying their extended families. Richard, at age sixteen, played football, participated in school plays and chorus and was popular with friends at high school and in youth group.

Peggy and Kathy had sleepovers with cousins and friends. They took piano lessons and attended summer church camp.

Little brother Tim was a well-behaved, creative four-year-old who idolized his big brother and sisters.

In 1964, Glenn and Treva have the perfect family.

Almost.

Until this day, March 4, 1964.

Suddenly, Treva finds herself interrupting Glenn's workday. Her mission—to tell him she is taking their second child to the hospital.

"The doctors are very alarmed," she tries to explain calmly. She takes a breath and continues, "They don't sound too hopeful," she adds, fighting back the flood of emotion that squeezes her heart and heaves her stomach. Maybe, she hopes, Glenn will excuse himself from work. Maybe he will see she cannot go through this frightening uncertainty alone.

But his strong Pennsylvania Dutch work ethic wins out.

His lower lip quivering and his hands gentle on her shoulders, he instructs, "You take her out to the hospital. By the time she is settled in her room, I'll be finished here and then I'll find you there."

Treva bravely concedes.

Arm around her, Glenn accompanies his young wife out through the gray mist to the car parked in front. How many times had he lightly trod down this street to the farmers' market for lunchtime distraction? Now, his steps are heavy and sullen.

As he approaches the car, his beautiful daughter waits in her tentative prison. He puts on a smile.

I roll down the window.

"So you're on a new adventure, huh, princess?"

"I guess so." The racing cars in my stomach shift into high gear.

"Well. We must trust the Lord to make everything all right. He'll give the doctors the answers to make you feel better." His soft brown eyes look a little wet to me.

"But I hope I don't have to miss school, Daddy. The big basketball game with York Suburban is this weekend." I am a good cheerleader. "The guys need all of us to get the crowd yelling." I am good at creating enthusiasm.

"We'll have to wait and see what happens, okay?"

Daddy reaches through the window and takes my hand. I can see little droplets collecting on his hair and eyebrows.

"I'll come out to the hospital right after work, in a couple of hours. Okay, sweetie?"

"Okay, Daddy. I'm kind of scared though."

"Mommy is here with you. And remember your Bible verse? 'He careth for you.'"

"Yes, I remember."

I had memorized Bible verses since I was five years old. Maybe even younger. Each child earned gold star stickers on a paper to reward them for learning the verses on the little blue tickets they received each week for attending Sunday school. Some of the words didn't mean much to me. But every now and then, there was a verse that I could understand. This was one of them. I was wondering, however, "If God cares for me, then why must I go to the hospital?"

"Everything's going to be all right." And when Daddy said it, I knew it had to be true. "I love you, princess," and he bends down and kisses my forehead.

Mother starts the car, as Daddy steps back from the curb.

"See you soon?" She looks over me out the passenger window.

"In a little bit," and he throws her a kiss.

CHAPTER 7

Terrors of Hospital Life

W as it because it was 1964 and York Hospital had no pediatrics ward? Or because this never before seen ailment was so complicated? Or because the doctors were uncertain of its contagion, uncertain if I was contagious and could infect others, especially children?

For whatever reason, I was admitted to a semi-private room on the internal medicine floor. The patient sharing this room with me had already been hospitalized for several weeks. She was ninety-one years old, and from what I could see, just a little pile of bed linens. Mrs. Brown could not communicate. I was uncertain if that was because the old lady was so weak or in a semi-coma or just because she was inhibited by all the medical hardware she was attached to. There were tubes going in and tubes coming out of the tiny woman. The room was filled with the constant sound of machines beeping and hissing and swishing.

Mrs. Brown was in the bed next to the window. The curtain between the two beds was kept drawn shut most of the time. My side of the room was in perpetual shadow. An omen of my upcoming days.

I had never been in a hospital before. In 1964, there were strict rules prohibiting children under age twelve from visiting hospital care units unless they were patients. None of my relatives or friends were ever hospitalized, and if they were, it was not discussed in front of me. Occasionally, I may have heard my mother and my aunts chat about their experiences in the hospital when they had had their babies. But even that was just mostly about the food or a nurse or how glad they were to return home. So going in, I was quite mortified.

Mother stayed with me through the admitting process and into the afternoon until suppertime.

"I'm going downstairs now to meet Daddy," she finally said after I was settled into my bed. "We'll grab a little something for supper. Then we'll come back here."

"Okay," I said reluctantly as I opened my journal to a fresh clean page. "I'll be fine," I lied as I searched the nightstand for my pen.

"Eat your dinner now," she urged, walking out the door.

The beeping, hissing, and swishing of the machines behind the curtain was all that broke the utter stillness of this cramped new world.

I found my pen, and my fear and tears spilled onto the page.

March 4, 1964

Dear Kim,

You'll never believe it! I am in the hospital!

It's pretty scary. My roommate is a zombie, poor lady. Her daughter and son-in-law are here to visit now. I don't think she knows it, though. I hear them talking, but I don't think they are talking to her, probably to each other. I wonder if she even knows they are here.

Oh, well. I will pray for her.

Suppertime. I really don't feel like eating. Especially this stuff. I lifted the metal cover that keeps the food warm. Yuk! It looks like it's supposed to be some kind of meat, maybe liver. The smell is disgusting. If that's not bad enough, beside it, there is a pile of soggy-looking spinach,

fresh from the can. I thought maybe I'd try the mashed potatoes, but now I just feel like gagging.
Maybe I'll eat the red Jell-O and drink the milk.

Later,
Peggy

My writing is interrupted when a white-capped nurse with glasses and a blue cardigan sweater swoops into the room. I guess these people don't have to knock on the door first.

"Why aren't you eating your dinner, honey?" Her eyeglasses pinch her long nose between close-set beady eyes. "You have these sheets in a jumbled mess!"

Without hesitation, she straightens the stiff covers and sheets over me, stuffs them under the foot of the bed, so I can barely move my feet under their tightness. She wheels the tray table holding my dinner over my bed and lifts the metal dome covering the plate.

"M-m-m," she hums. "Look at that. Liver and spinach. You must eat all of it because you want to get well, don't you?"

My stomach heaves at the smell wafting up my nose!

I go through the motions of lifting my fork and spreading the napkin over the front of my hospital gown. Slowly, I scoop a forkful of potatoes and draw it to my mouth. I'm hoping to convince her that she has accomplished her mission here, so she scurries out the door.

Instead, she bustles to the other side of the room, cooing over the unhearing Mrs. Brown.

"You're lucky you're in here out of the rain today, honey."

She may as well be talking to the wall.

I quickly stuff a few forkfuls of food into a corner of my napkin and scrape the remainder to the side of the plate. Maybe the bare spot in the middle will give the impression I have consumed a portion of the green and white mush.

"Oh, my! What have you done?" the raspy voice comes from the other side of the curtain. The beeping of machines is now interrupted by a shuffling and rattle of the collecting bucket hit by plastic tubing, then the sustained squeal of a flat-lining heart monitor.

Suddenly, there are other nurses rushing in, green uniformed attendants drawing curtains around the foot of my bed, as identical green uniforms push a cart into the room. Voices tumble over one another.

"Disconnect that, so I can get in here," urges one.

"Can you lift that thing out of the way?"

"Well, let's hope this works."

"What happened?"

"Maybe we should try atropine."

"Not without Dr. Jamison's orders."

"Okay, get that thing out of here. We'll have to move her."

"Get a gurney."

I don't want to be here. I shove the tray table away and pull the covers over my head. What a nightmare! Where are Mother and Daddy? Maybe they'll take me home when they hear about this!

What am I being punished for? Is it because I've had jealous thoughts about my pretty friend, Carolyn? Or because, down deep, I've been angry with Mrs. Stein, my gym teacher, for keeping me on the bench during intramural volleyball games? Oh, how I wish I could jump backward in time. Be a different person. Take back some things I've said. Have a better attitude. Why can't I be like the perfect girls in my Grace Livingston Hill novels?

By now, the excitement on the other side of the room has subsided. The machines on that side of the curtain are making their former steady beeping, swishing, and hissing.

When it seems quiet enough, I slowly come out from under my hiding place. I guess Nurse Nasty has forgotten about me in the crisis next to me.

I reach into the top drawer of my bedstand and pull out my soft black leather-covered Bible. The book opens to a well-read passage, Romans 8:38, KJV. "For I am persuaded that neither death nor life, nor angels nor principalities nor powers, nor things present nor things to come, shall be able to separate us from the love of God which is in Christ Jesus." Reading the verse over and over, I begin whispering the words to commit them to memory. Gradually, the gentle lull of their familiarity soothes my nerves.

"Knock. Knock."

A comforting voice accompanies gentle rapping on the heavy wooden door. My pretty red-haired mother followed by my tall debonair daddy enter carrying a shopping bag and a flower arrangement of bright yellow daffodils and delicate purple grape hyacinths, what we always called bluebells. I am instantly transported to the cow pasture on my friend's farm: a cool spring day as we tip-toe around the manure piles in order to collect bouquets of sunshine and jewels.

Mother sits on the side of my bed. I hope she hasn't noticed my quick swipe across the eyes or my sniffling. I know she is hoping her little girl can get through a few days in the hospital without too much trauma or discomfort.

"We got you some surprises," she attempts to create a party-like anticipation.

Daddy comes close to embrace me. "How are you doing, Princess?"

His smiling gentle tone sweeps over me like a warm blanket.

"I'm doing okay," I cling to his broad shoulders an extra moment. "I'm not sick enough to be in the hospital." I lower my voice to a whisper. "Not sick like Mrs. Brown over there."

My fright hangs uncontrollably on the edge of my emotions.

"Just before you came, I felt like I was in that TV show, *Ben Casey*."

And the story of bustling nurses giving nervous orders tumbles out of me.

One of my most persistent traits is my impulsiveness. More often than not, I speak before thinking how my words might impact the hearer.

Treva and Glenn were not at all pleased that their daughter had been placed in a room with an old woman on the brink of death. They wanted to surround her with life and hope. Treva wished she could take Peggy's place. A little girl so full of potential shouldn't have to be cooped up like this. She wanted her daughter's hospital stay to be as brief and pleasant as possible.

Glenn's world had been mightily shaken in the last four hours, also. Doctors and hospitals held no place in his life. Growing up as one of seven children in the Great Depression, sickness in his family was treated with home remedies of teas and broths and cold packs. The only

47

time a doctor was summoned was when someone was dying or perhaps being born.

Now, here was his beautiful daughter confined to a sterile hospital bed, talking of doctors and bedpans and needles. The place smelled like medicine and sickness. It was all he could do to keep from gagging.

So silently, he prayed.

He prayed for the health of his daughter, for the skill and wisdom of the doctors, and for strength for him and his dear wife to face whatever may be ahead.

"I brought you some after dinner mints." Daddy smiles warmly, offering me a blue paper-wrapped roll of peppermint Lifesavers.

"What good things did you have for dinner?" Mother asks cheerily.

I nearly choke as I describe my unappetizing entree. Then, I add, "I drank all my milk and ate my Jell-O. I tasted a little bit of everything." I am quickly learning to assure my parents that I am really okay here.

It seems as if Mother and Daddy have been here only a few minutes when a voice comes through speakers in the hallway. "The time is now 8:20. Visiting hours end in ten minutes."

The bottom drops out of my stomach. I suddenly feel full of panic and fear.

"Will you come tomorrow, Mommy and Daddy?"

"Of course," Mother assures me.

"I'll come right after work, Princess," Daddy chimes in.

"Do you want to put on a pair of your new pajamas?"

Mother pulls three sets of brightly colored nightwear from the shopping bags. She hates leaving her little girl in this strange place. Maybe something new will make it more bearable.

"Yes. The pretty green-checked ones. I really like them." I cling to each remaining moment with my company.

Mother pulls the curtain to provide privacy. Then she helps me shed the dumpy hospital gown and climb into the brightly checkered cotton pajamas.

"These embroidered strawberries are so pretty," I express my delight. Then Mother pulls the curtain open again.

"The time is now 8:30," bellows the hallway speaker. "Visiting hours are over."

I move toward Daddy and throw my arms around his neck. "I wish you didn't have to leave," I beg.

"I know, sweetie," he returns softly. "I wish we could take you with us. But you sleep quick, and before you know it, tomorrow will be here."

As I turn to Mother, I catch her swiping away some tears.

"Can I tuck you in?" Mother asks quickly. "It will be nice and quiet and you can read for a while."

I hop into bed. Mother tucks the covers around me.

"I hear they get you up pretty early around here." She smooths my reddish brown hair. "You have a good night and we'll see you tomorrow." She kisses my forehead.

I pull Mother close and kiss her cheek. "Okay," I try to steady my trembling voice.

Mother gathers her purse and coat. She and Daddy reluctantly step to the door. And with one last whispered "Good night," I see their smiling faces turn and leave.

I feel as if I have been clinging to a rope suspended above a lake. Slowly, my fingers begin to slip until finally they lose their grip and I am plunging toward the water. Now I am alone, and it is up to me to sink or swim. I immediately sink, burying my face into my pillow as I sob and sob.

CHAPTER 8

A Parent's Worst Nightmare

G lenn and Treva walk out of the hospital to the parking lot in silence. Since they each have a car in the lot, they part as Glenn says gently, "I'll see you at home."

Driving down the highway, Treva wonders about the people behind the headlights coming toward her and speeding past. Are they going home to their healthy families after a long day at work? Are they taking their kids home after a basketball game? Are they driving with their entire family in the car on their way home from mid-week church services?

"Dear God. Do you see us now? What is the purpose of this? Are you punishing me for something? Have I taken you for granted? I have tried so hard to be a good wife and mother. What have I done to make Peggy sick? Maybe I haven't cleaned the dishes thoroughly. Maybe my kitchen is dirtier than I think. I so wish it would be me and not Peggy in the hospital. Please be with her, God. Keep her safe. If you will, please make a miracle and heal her. I'll try to be better in every way."

Meanwhile, Glenn is praying in the same way. This is all so bewildering. How will he pay for these medical bills? How long will Peggy be kept in the hospital? What will happen in her school progress? When and what will they tell the other children?

Suddenly, he realizes he does not know how long he has been stopped at the end of the highway exit ramp. He wipes his forehead with his palm and slowly turns left onto the road leading past his rural home.

The little brick church sits primly at the top of the hill. At the stop sign there, Glenn rolls down his window and lets the brisk March air sweep over him. He cannot breathe in deeply enough to consume the sweet green brew. If only it could cleanse away all the turmoil inside.

He parks his 1959 Dodge in the gravel driveway. Then, he walks across the road to the mailbox for the daily paper and other mail. There is no moon tonight. No stars either. The clouded darkness makes this night even blacker than usual.

Inside the warmly lit house, Treva urges Richard and Kathy to organize their school books for tomorrow morning. She leads four-and-a-half-year-old Timmy to the bathroom to wash his face, neck, ears, and hands. Then, helps him dress in his pajamas.

Glenn enters the back door just as Timmy is about to climb the stairs. The young father lays the mail and his lunch box on the kitchen counter and swoops up the little boy in his arms.

"Time for bed, cowboy?" He holds the little guy close for a long moment.

"Yep," and then, "Daddy, let go! I can't breathe!"

Glenn kisses him on the cheek and carefully lowers him to the floor.

"Oops. Sorry, soldier. I got carried away. Up the wooden hill with you. Good night." And he ruffles the hair of his miniature self.

Before long, the older children retreat to their rooms for bedtime reading. The house seems deadly quiet as Treva and Glenn finally sink into their accustomed living room chairs. But instead of reading the newspaper as usual, they find themselves staring blankly through the pages.

Glenn has turned several pages before he realizes he remembers none of what he has just looked at, read, scanned.

Treva just sits silently, her eyes closed.

This day has lasted a lifetime. Nothing will ever be the same.

CHAPTER 9

Semantics: Hold Breakfast

I awaken very early the next morning to the unfamiliar sounds of nurses speaking at full volume in the hallway.

"Oh, yes. I remember. I am in the hospital. These sheets aren't as soft as the ones on my bed at home."

I rub my eyes to adjust to the dimly lit room. Dawn is just breaking and the curtain between my bed and Mrs. Brown's is pulled closed, so daylight barely enters.

"Maybe I'll read my Bible a little bit. That should make me feel better."

And I reach to the bedside cabinet to open the top drawer where I had placed my few personal belongings. There, on the very drawer I am about to open, is a wide tape with large letters reading, *HOLD BREAKFAST*.

"Oh, dear. I thought I could put stuff in this drawer. But I guess this tray is for my breakfast. Will I ever get used to these hospital ways?"

So dutifully, I lift each item from the drawer—Lifesaver mints that Daddy gave me, my Bible, my journal, and pen, a comb and hairbrush—and place them in the cabinet below, all but the Bible which I keep on my lap.

"There. That should do it. The tray is empty now. It can hold my breakfast."

I begin reading one of my favorite Psalms. It is difficult to concentrate because I am constantly aware of the voices in the hallway, wondering if someone will be coming into my room.

And sure enough, before long, in comes a man wearing a white coat and a big smile. He flips the wall switch inside the door, which turns on the bright lights over the bed.

"Good morning, little lady! How are you doing today?"

Before I have a chance to answer, he sits on the edge of the bed. "I'm Dick. I'm going to take a little blood from you so the doctors can figure out how to make you better."

"Okay."

With gentle but practiced hands, Dick ties a tourniquet around my upper arm. "Now let's just hold this arm out nice and straight."

Without hesitation, he quickly prepares a hematology syringe and preps the arm with a swipe of alcohol. Just at the part of the arm that bends, he finds a blue vein and warns, "Get ready for a little pinch."

But almost before he says it, he has the needle in my arm and is drawing blood—one, two, three—six tubes of blood! He gently withdraws the needle, places a cotton ball and a Band-Aid on my arm where it has been pierced, and disposes of the syringe and other accessories in a little orange bin hanging on the wall marked *bio-hazard*. As he removes his plastic gloves and gathers his little carrier, he smiles.

"Oh, I guess we can get rid of this now, too." He reaches for the tape reading, *HOLD BREAKFAST*, tears it off with a swoop, and throws it and his gloves into the trash can.

"You have a nice day, sweetie!" and he leaves the room.

Soon after he has gone, a little lady dressed in blue enters with a tray. She places it on the wheeled table next to my bed and guides the table over top of my legs.

"Here's your breakfast. They already took your blood, right?"

"Yes. Thank you." This is how I am learning hospital speak. "Hold breakfast" means "Patient must fast until blood is drawn." How my world is changing!

53

Friday, March 6, 1964

Dear Kim,

Today, they moved me across and down the hall into a different room. I have a bed next to the window and the whole room is much brighter.

My new roommate had a gall bladder operation. She is very sweet. A little older than Mother, maybe. It's just nice to have a living, breathing person around instead of a specter of death! That other room was like something from the Twilight Zone!

Rev. Wright was here to visit me this morning. He left just a few minutes ago. He is so nice. He read a little bit of scripture to me—the story about the woman in the crowd who knew that if she could just touch the edge of Jesus's robe, she could be healed. And then, wow, Jesus actually felt healing power go out of his body! Is that weird?

I don't know if my faith is strong enough to be healed. The strange thing is I really don't feel all that bad. A little tired maybe.

The doctors, Dr. Knoch and some younger intern doctor, came to my room this morning. They said I am a very sick girl. That I should take the medicine the nurses bring and do as they say.

All I want is to get out of here and go back to school. Today is the day Richard F. has lunch the same time as me. I missed seeing him in the cafeteria. Sometimes, we even just happen to be in line together and can talk a little. Oh, well. Maybe next week. I can't wait!

Love,
Peggy

Sunday, March 8, 1964

Dear Kim,

You wouldn't believe what a busy weekend I've had! Lots of visitors. That's the best part of being in the hospital. And cards. I got seven get-well cards on Saturday— from Grandma Whorl, Aunt Mary, a couple of Mother's customers, Mr. and Mrs. Moramarco, Sarah and Bob Snyder, and, my favorite, the Flemmens family!

One of the bad things about being here is the blood tests. Every morning around 5:30, someone comes through the door and flips on the light switch. What a way to wake up! You're finally sleeping soundly, and suddenly, this glaring brightness floods your dream land. Then, before you're fully awake, they're tying a pinching tourniquet around your arm and stabbing you with a needle which they let in your arm until they suck out at least ten test tubes full of blood. Then they say, "Okay, you can go back to sleep now."

Okay. Sure.

The noise in the hallway begins around 6:30 a.m. I think that's when night nurses are telling day nurses what happened in the night, the condition of patients, and maybe what to expect in the day.

For me, it's no use trying to go back to sleep, so I just read my Bible and pray and maybe write a letter.

Yawn. I'm feeling pretty sleepy now. Talk to you tomorrow.

Love,
Peggy

Monday, March 9, 1964

Dear Kim,

The day started off slowly enough. I even liked my breakfast—French toast and orange juice and bacon.

My roommate, Mrs. Hake, is excited about going home tomorrow so she's all bright and chipper.

But, right after the nurse gave me my basin bath, someone showed up at the door with a wheelchair. They wheeled it beside my bed and practically lifted me into it. They don't want me to walk around much.

Oh, I guess I forgot to tell you.

Thursday, the first full day I was here, still over in Mrs. Brown's room, I was so bored. So I got out of bed and rearranged things in my bedstand, then I walked a few steps from the bed to the dresser so I could look more closely at the daffodils and blue bells Mother brought me. Nurse Nasty came barging in, squealing, "What do you think you're doing, young lady? You are not to get out of that bed except to go to the bathroom! Don't you know how sick you are?"

I wanted to crawl in a hole. No one told me to stay in bed, and no, I didn't think I was very sick at all.

So anyway, that's why a nurse and this little old wheelchair guy lifted me into this wheelchair. Then, the wheelchair driver pushed me to the elevators and down hallways until we finally ended up where they take x-rays. I don't know how many they took! "Lay here. Roll over. Hold your breath. Roll over on your other side. Put your arms up over your head. No, just stretch them up. That's right. Now, hold your breath. Okay. Breathe." And over and over again.

All done at last!

What an adventure!

By the time I got back to my room, it was lunchtime.

Mrs. Hake said, "You were gone a long time. I thought maybe you left me," she chuckled.

Ooops! Gotta go. Looks like there's another adventure on the way.

I'm glad you're here for me, Kim. This really is kind of scary.

Love,
Peggy

CHAPTER 10

Breaking the News

I n this unexpected collision with phenomena out of their grasp, Treva and Glenn struggled to maintain some kind of control.

One morning, on the Saturday after I was admitted to the hospital, they gathered their other three children, Richard, Kathy and Timmy, around the coffee table in their little living room. Guardedly, they attempted to explain that Peggy was very sick, much more sick than anyone had imagined. They did not know how long she might be in the hospital.

"But," they continued, "we believe God is taking care of your sister. And we can help by praying. So let's do that now."

Glenn prayed, thanking God for all the good gifts this family enjoyed—shelter, food, work, good schools, and good friends. He even gave thanks for good health.

Then he thanked God for his great love and for the forgiveness of sins through the love of Jesus Christ.

Glenn took a deep breath and his voice trembled a little when he prayed, "Dear Lord, please be with Peggy right now. This is a very difficult time for us. We don't understand why she has become so ill. But, dear Lord, we know that you are the Master of everything and we pray that you will reach out and heal her, give her strength and, most of all, give her faith. We hold her up to you and ask a miracle. Be with the doctors and give them insight and wisdom to help Peggy get better every day.

"We believe you have a special plan in this, Lord.

"We thank you for your mercy.

"In your blessed name we pray. Amen."

Treva spoke next.

"Remember, God loves us and we can talk to him any time at all."

The children sat quietly for a moment. Then, Kathy and Tim went outside to play with the cats and dogs. Richard went back upstairs to his room to read.

Treva and Glenn clasped each other's hands in a moment of silent desperation.

CHAPTER 11

Threats

When my parents visited me Monday evening, I clung to them like ivy to a tree's trunk. I told them that a doctor, an intern, had stopped by during the day when I was alone to tell me, "We may decide to do a liver biopsy. That's when we take a small piece of your liver to study it and try to find out what is making you sick or just how damaged the liver might be."

"I don't want to be cut open, Mommy. Can't you just take me home?"

Treva shot a worried glance at Glenn. Then, she comforted me as best she could. "Now, don't you worry. They won't do anything without our permission. Really, they should have talked to us first before they said anything to you. But you don't have to think about that now, Peggy."

As she hugged me close, she looked up at Glenn with pleading eyes.

"So who else came to see you today, Princess? Was Reverend Wright here?" Glenn plopped loosely into the chair at the foot of the bed.

Releasing from Mother's embrace, I answered with a smile, "Yes, he was here. And Sarah came at around 11:30 this morning. She said she had just donated some blood. So since it was lunch time and they always put coffee on my tray, she drank that and we split the cookie that was dessert."

Scooting over to my nightstand, I erupted, "Oh! And look at all the pretty get-well cards I got!"

I presented a handful of envelopes to Mother, who was sitting on the side of the bed.

As Treva opened each card, read it, and announced its sender, she passed it to Glenn, who returned it to me. Thoughts of the biopsy faded as I soaked up the bright colors of painted flowers and animals on each card.

Aunt Mary and Uncle Charlie knocked at the door. They showered me with smiles and kisses. As Aunt Mary was placing a basket of pink and yellow flowers on the window sill, yet another knock was heard on the open door.

This time, it was Dr. Knoch in his mousy gray suit with his matching gray squinty little eyes and a white-coated intern at his side. They shuffled their way in and immediately began drawing the curtains around the bed.

"Excuse us for a moment. You can wait outside," Dr. Knoch ordered the visitors.

I thought he was awfully bossy for such a little guy.

He told me to lie down and lifted my pajama top just far enough for him to tap on my swollen abdomen. He also pressed in gently with his fingertips, first on the right side, then the left.

"There. You can feel it easily. The liver and the spleen."

Then, the intern also tapped and pressed.

Dr. Knoch placed his stethoscope in his ears, leaned over me, and placed the cold listening device onto my belly.

"Take a deep breath and blow it out." He moved the stethoscope. "Again." He repeated this several times and I obeyed. As uncomfortable as I was exposing myself like this, what else could I do?

"Okay. Your visitors can come back now." Dr. Knoch smiled evilly. "We'll see you tomorrow." And he patted my leg through the sheets as they turned and left.

Uncle Charlie was first back in the room with a chuckle and a grin. "Boy, those doctors sure don't keep no banker's hours, do they?" His crisp Pennsylvania German accent always cheered me. "I'll bet they wake ya' up just when you're gettin' good sleepin', too!"

Soon, Aunt Mary and Treva and Glenn joined him, surrounding my bed and chattering away about starting the vegetable garden and did you hear about old man Rohrbaugh? He just about got stuck in the chicken coop with that big ol' guinea hen again!

All too soon, the laughter and fun were interrupted by the dreadful announcement, "Visiting hours are concluded."

Once again, there were hugs and kisses, farewells and promises of another visit soon. Strange how the room that was dancing in glorious laughter and fun at eight o'clock, that same evening at nine o'clock should turn so deathly still and cold.

CHAPTER 12

Lab Specimen

The next day would be seared into my memory forever. It began routinely enough—blood drawn, breakfast, bath in bed, and room cleaning. Then, along came the wheelchair again. In my first three days in the hospital, I had made several wheelchair trips to the x-ray department.

My thirteen-year-old spirits were high that day. Still glowing in the pleasant memory of the visit with my parents and aunt and uncle from the night before, I had chosen to wear my favorite green cotton pajamas. The day was cloudy and the bright green and white pattern splashed with delicate red embroidery and crisp white rick-rack was like a flower in the rain. Maybe I could brighten the day for lots of other sick people today.

I greeted the candy striper pushing the wheelchair with a smile, "Good morning!"

But instead of the now familiar route to x-ray, my ride through the hospital corridors and elevators ended in a classroom with desk chairs full of interns—at least twenty young men in white coats.

Two of them lifted me from the wheelchair onto a gurney in the front of the classroom. As I lay there, the only people I recognized were my internist Dr. Knoch and the hospital pathologist, Dr. McKeon, who had examined me when I was admitted a few days before. One or two of the interns looked vaguely familiar, probably from accompanying Dr. Knoch on his brief visits to my room.

It really didn't matter. I was not addressed as a person in this situation. As Dr. McKeon spoke to the group, I gradually realized that me and my mysterious disorder was the lesson of the day. As moments crept by, I found myself clenching my teeth. My hands had formed tight fists by my side.

After a few opening remarks, Dr. McKeon invited the interns to come forward to feel the enlarged liver and swollen spleen in the specimen before them. Indelicately, he unbuttoned the pretty green-checked top of my pajamas, laying bare my torso from neck to navel. I closed my eyes as, with a ball-point pen, he drew on the skin of my abdomen, outlining my enlarged liver and spleen. Then, the parade of interns began. Each one stopped to prod first the right, then the left side of my abdomen.

I was so embarrassed. My young developing breasts were exposed to everyone. How carefully modest I had been in the locker room at school. Even in front of the girls in my class, I was uncomfortable in my bra and panties.

Now, here I lay, totally topless in front of twenty young men, strangers, who were touching me one by one. It didn't help me to think that they were doctors and that the body was their business.

My only hope was to escape. To pretend this wasn't happening to me.

I silently recited to myself over and over again the twenty-third Psalm, "The Lord is my shepherd. I shall not want. He makes me lay down in green pastures. He leads me beside still waters. He restores my soul. Even though I may walk through the valley of death, I will fear no evil, for God is with me. God's rod and staff comfort me. God prepares a table before me in the presence of my enemies. God anoints my head with oil. Surely, goodness and mercy shall follow me all the days of my life and I will dwell in the house of the Lord forever...the Lord is my shepherd I shall not want" (my own translation).

Over and over, I repeated the scripture in my mind to remove myself further and further from this present horror.

Finally, twenty-five minutes after it began, the relay of prodding interns ended. Dr. Knoch told me, "You can button your pj's again."

I blinked back tears as I fumbled to do as he said. Seemingly oblivious to my trauma, he continued his lecture to the roomful of white coats.

I remained on the gurney, eyes closed. I did not want to see the men who had seen me and touched me. After what seemed like hours to me, I was back in my room in the hospital bed surrounded by colorful get-well cards and spring flower arrangements. On my nightstand lay a little pile of newly arrived envelopes. My hands trembled as I reached for them. Unprompted tears rolled down my cheeks as I privately opened each one, reading the names of friends and relatives I wondered if I'd ever see again.

That evening, when supper came, I ignored it. I didn't watch television. I didn't read or write. I hardly spoke to anyone, except when it was absolutely necessary. Even when Mother and Daddy came to visit, I spoke very little.

"I want to go home now," I whispered.

"Maybe next weekend, Princess," Daddy soothed.

This was only Tuesday. I said nothing. After today's experience, I was terrified to imagine what the next few days might hold for me.

During the visit, Dr. Knoch and Dr. McKeon passed by my door. I thought I heard them speaking as they lingered just outside in the corridor.

Just about that time, my cousin Cynthia entered the room with an armful of books. As she began presenting them one by one to me, Mother and Daddy stepped out into the hallway.

Cynthia had brought a couple of Nancy Drew mysteries, a collection of crossword puzzles, and a book of poetry by Emily Dickinson. We chatted about our favorite books and TV shows. I asked Cynthia how her flute practice was going and was marching band all finished for the year?

Cynthia, always the curious biologist, asked questions about my diagnosis and treatment. I had very few answers except one, "The doctors don't know yet. They keep saying, 'We think it might have been an infectious hepatitis, but is not now. Or maybe the inflammation was caused by a virus and just never went away after the virus was subdued. Whatever happened, it really destroyed a great deal of the liver.' So I guess no one really knows what's wrong. They did say that the liver is the only organ in the body capable of regenerating itself."

Then we laughed together as I shared some of my cards and lighter unusual experiences since I'd been hospitalized. Like the day I was chewing gum and the good-natured orderly came in to clean my room.

"I suddenly realized my gum wasn't in my mouth anymore. So I told him, 'Watch out where you walk. I think I dropped some gum on the floor.' In his bright blue coveralls, he looked and looked. He got down on his knees and looked under the bed. 'All that's under here are some dust balls and a couple 'a pink slippers,' he chuckled. Then he stood and grabbed his mop. I started looking through my sheets. It was a mystery to me.

"Then, after he left the room, what a sweet little guy, I found the gum stuck to my pajamas! It seemed so funny that we spent all that time looking for it. And he was just so cute, searching everywhere."

Meanwhile, out in the hallway, the doctors, McKeon and Knoch, were informing my parents of what they were guessing about their daughter's condition. There was definitely something awry with her liver. The levels of bilirubin her bloodstream indicated a great deal of damage. Also, the fact that her liver and spleen were so unusually enlarged pointed to disease it would have been better to discover much earlier. They could not say what caused this, whether it began as an infectious form of hepatitis and then just lingered and smoldered or was caused by a viral infection. They had never encountered anything like this before. But they thought a regimen of high-dose steroid treatment to curb further inflammation and perhaps intense nourishment along with complete bed rest may extend the youngster's life a few weeks.

"We really can't predict how long she will last. It could be days. It could be a couple of months. We'd like to examine her a bit more and see how she reacts to the drugs. But we can't promise anything."

Shortly after Mother and Daddy came back into the room, Cynthia had to leave to go home and do a homework assignment.

Mother looked worried. Daddy spoke first, "Any visitors today?"

"No. Well. There was a note here from Nelda Mae after I returned to the room around four o'clock. It says she'll come again another time," I explained, handing the note to Daddy. Evading the details, I added, "I was out for a while and must have missed her."

Mother had a brown paper bag clutched in her hand. She stared absently into the air. I broke her trance, saying, "What's in the bag, Mommy?"

Treva was startled back to the hospital room. She handed the bag to me.

"Just a little something to keep you company."

I pulled out of the bag a soft stuffed animal. The little lamb wore a pink ribbon around its neck and had blue glass eyes. Its white fleece felt warm as I cuddled the comforting toy close.

"Oooh! I love it! Thank you, thank you, thank you!" And as I clasped the lamb in one arm, I reached out to Mother with the other.

Treva held her daughter close for a lingering moment. She was happy that Peggy found such joy in this little gift.

During the remainder of the visit, I showed Mother and Daddy the books Cynthia had delivered to me. Mother told me of all the get-well wishes she received from several customers and other friends. Daddy said he had seen Mr. Nolan, one of the junior high school football coaches, in the hardware store and he had asked how I was faring.

Once again, visiting hours ended much sooner than I wanted. I tried hard not to cry as Mother and Daddy waved, "Good night."

CHAPTER 13

Death Sentence

After fourteen days in the hospital, Dr. Knoch and Dr. McKeon decided there was nothing more to be done to save me. So they prescribed a regimen of eighty milligrams of prednisone per day and a high carbohydrate, high protein diet. The doctors instructed Mother to feed me two eggs and a half-pound of meat each day, which would hopefully provide enough protein to regenerate the liver, at least partially. Unbeknownst to me, they told my parents that perhaps I would survive another month or so. The diet would be supplemented with a high-protein milkshake, Meritene. With this prescribed fuel, administered twice a day, my body should have substantial building blocks to extend life a bit longer.

If I survived another month, I would be brought to the hospital for blood work. My liver function tests would be evaluated and the doctors would examine me.

"We'll go from there," Dr. Knoch said with his benign smirk.

And so, since this was all that the doctor had to offer, my mother and father wordlessly vowed to create a miracle. They would immerse their precious daughter in faith and hope.

CHAPTER 14

Homecoming

At last! I'm going home! To the beautiful little room I share with my sister, with its eave-sloping ceiling, the mirrored dresser where half of the surface holds her stuff and half holds mine... little trinkets we call our own. Each of us had received a jewelry box from Aunt Mamie for our birthday. It plays music when it is opened. Kathy's sits centrally, on her side of the dresser, the left side. Mine is on the right. We carefully placed on the white tatted dresser scarf, little objects that meant something to us as individuals. Kathy positioned in front of her black jewelry box a few smooth-washed colored stones she had found along the stream near our cabin in the mountains. I had placed a blue jay's feather I brought home from church camp last year beside a tiny tube of orange blossom cream perfume Mother bought for me on a trip with friends to Florida.

The original 1929 wallpaper still surrounded us there in our little haven. Red and orange-hatted elves crouched beside brightly polka-dotted toadstools. Blue dragonflies and jumping green frogs peppered the spaces. Although the reds and greens and blues had slightly faded against the beige background over the years, these fantastical figures were so much a part of my home and comfort.

As I departed my hospital room, the starched white nurse helped me into a wheelchair.

"Oh, I'm sure I can walk," I protested.

"Maybe so. But we'd rather give you a ride to the door."

The smile in her voice seemed somehow practiced, something she said every day.

The ride home in the car brought a bundle of sensations. It was comforting to once again hear Mother and Daddy's casual conversation in the front seat. The movement of the vehicle over the pavement felt like a new and frightening experience. The whole world seemed a wonder—trees pushing out the tiniest leaves, a wash of new green everywhere. Cars rushing past, people walking here and there.

Don't they know Death is just lurking around the corner?

Birds sit congregated on telephone wires. A bunny scampers through a yard.

Ahhhh. I am returning to life as it should be.

As Daddy pulls the car into our gravel driveway, Mother queries, "Are you ready for your hike up the steps?"

After two weeks in a hospital bed, I am anxious for a hike down our country roads!

"Oh, yes, Mommy. I'm sure I'll have no problem."

Daddy gathers a few things I have accumulated during my hospital stay. Mother gingerly helps me from the back seat of the red and white Dodge, across the bridge and up the thirteen steps beside the house leading to the back door.

"Where are Kathy and Rich and Tim?" I am excited to see my brothers and sister again after two weeks away from them.

"Oh, Kathy and Rich are still in school. Tim is spending the day at Lanny's. He'll be home close to suppertime. Meanwhile, we'll get you all settled in."

Daddy comes through the back door. "Welcome home, Princess. We put this bed in the living room so you won't have to go up and down the stairs."

I am disappointed that I won't soon be returning to my little elf-inhabited bedroom. However, it is a relief to sit on the edge of the single bed, actually fatigued from the short climb up the outside steps.

It was March 18, 1964. Fourteen days had passed since I last felt the warmth of home. Reality seemed like a dream. The large doses of prednisone made me feel distant and removed. Almost like I was experiencing life outside my own being.

CHAPTER 15

Sustaining Life

The parents prayed, the church people prayed, and members of the community prayed and expressed hope for the thirty-nine-year old parents. Classmates wrote letters.

Mrs. Shank, my beloved choral teacher, sent a tablet of lined newsprint paper all around the class. She asked each student to write a line or two to me, expressing get-well wishes. After adding her own encouraging note, she taped one page to another, then rolled up the final product forming a thick scroll. Over the next few days, the chorus class of thirteen-year-olds brought little packages wrapped in colorful paper and ribbons to school. The presents were notepads, stationery, a used book, coloring books and crayons, and other such tokens. These brightly wrapped gifts were carefully placed, along with the scroll into a cardboard box covered with wrapping paper. One day, in late afternoon, Mrs. Shank delivered the sunshine box to me. She explained that I could open one package each day until they were all unwrapped. She also presented the scroll to me, saying, "We miss you in chorus. We hope you will sing with us again soon."

Dear Mrs. Shank. She quickly wiped away a tear, and I wondered if she thought I may never return to school, much less sing with my friends again.

I puzzled what all the fuss was about, because I was certain I would be riding a bike in a few weeks. I would enjoy the summer sun and swim and hike through the woods. The hospital interruption was just an inconvenience.

In truth, it was much more than that. As the bustle continued, I began to think, *Something is terribly wrong. But I'm still living and breathing. Surely, this can't last forever.*

Daddy had placed a single bed in the living room where I would be in the hub of activity, as well as preventing me from climbing up and downstairs each day. He positioned a small aquarium within my view at the foot of the bed. Even while lying down, I could watch the activity of black mollies and guppies as they darted in and around water plants and tiny castles. The bed was placed beside a window, so I could watch life outside among the trees, as well. It was Easter, after all. The lilac bush just outside the window was loaded with heavy purple blossoms, and spring was on its way, bursting forth into new life!

I was numbed by all this attention. Often, I gazed out that window, seemingly nothing in my mind. Just the thought that this was the only moment I was living. No future. No dreams. Just lilacs. Lilacs blooming on the bush outside that window. Robins beginning to congregate. Little birds nesting among the fragrant lavender blossoms.

Whether or not they were conscious of it, Mother and Daddy surrounded me with life. Daddy had never allowed animals in the house before I got sick. Animals were meant to live outdoors—cats, dogs, chickens, anything that could not ask, "Where is the restroom?" However, now, four-year-old Tim received a little beagle puppy, Pal, who was permitted to stay in the house. He became a wonderful distraction for me. Although well-behaved, Pal provided his share of inconveniences. Since I was not permitted to get up out of bed, except to go to the bathroom on the other side of the living room, I kept all my belongings under the bed. There, easily accessible, were my stationery and pen, my ever-needed journal, and books loaned to me by good friends. One of these books was a hardbound copy of Catherine Marshall's *A Man Called Peter*, an inspiring story about Mrs. Marshall's husband, evangelist Peter Marshall, loaned to me by one of my favorite school teachers, Mrs. Newell.

One morning, after breakfast, I reached under the bed, hoping to read a bit before my bath. When I pulled out the thick book, I found one corner of the hardcover had been chewed beyond repair. Teachers had warned me often enough not to "dog-ear" pages. Pal did his part in "dog teething" the book.

Another morning came and, although it was early spring and the nights were still cool, as I awakened, I felt uncomfortably warm. The cause—Pal was snuggled cozily under my chin, his long beagle snout fitting just so across my neck. Could he have sensed I needed extra comfort?

My mother worked in her beauty shop two or three days a week. So she often received phone calls at home from customers to schedule appointments. Always, after she replaced the telephone receiver on the rotary phone, she told me, "Lucile asked about you. She said they are praying for you," or "That was Mr. O'Keefe, the township supervisor. He said you are in their thoughts and prayers." However unconsciously, my young parents were immersing me in Life, probably the best medicine I received.

Others also did their best to make life more pleasant for me. My mother's friends from the Farm Women Society sent me more than one sunshine box throughout these months while I was bedfast. Someone arranged a "hankie shower" for me. People sent get-well cards and tucked a beautifully colored or embroidered handkerchief inside. If good will defeats illness, certainly, I was on the winning side.

Liver disease is very enigmatic, like a termite quietly destroying a structure from within. The liver has no nerve endings, so as it is slowly corrupted, there is no pain except from surrounding structures that may be affected.

I did not know just how completely my world had diminished. I could not realize that I would be confined to bed in this little living room for three long months. At the tender age of thirteen, I was forced to think about the possibility of dying. My parents did everything in their power to give energy to living.

CHAPTER 16

Tutors

After two weeks at home and routine care established there, my academic education resumed. One day, Mother told me, "The school has arranged for a few tutors to come to the house to teach you. I know your algebra teacher, Mrs. Newell, will teach you English and math. I'm not sure who will be here for geography and science."

I breathed a sigh of relief. There were certain teachers I did not look forward to being alone with. My English teacher at school was a little man who reminded me of Washington Irving's Ichabod Crane from *The Legend of Sleepy Hollow*. His suit hung loosely on his frail frame. He was kind and gentle, but reeked of pipe smoke. As he sat on the front of his desk, legs crossed, elbow on his knee, he held his pipe, clenched in his teeth, unlit of course. The closer you sat to the front of the class, the more odiferous was your experience in English.

So when I heard that the jolly Mrs. Newell was to teach me English, I was overjoyed. Mrs. Newell made learning fun and relevant. She had already shown her students the practical use of algebra. "Three girls have an after-school pizza party. They have invited two boys to join them. They know there will be plenty of pizza for everyone. But they have only two sixteen-ounce bottles of soda. If they want enough soda for each person to drink eight ounces, how much more will they need?"

Besides making learning fun, Mrs. Newell was simply a very pleasant person—no makeup, just her own naturally rosy cheeks, sparkling blue eyes behind mother-of-pearl inlaid glasses, and a winning smile. Her own enthusiasm for algebra was contagious. Additionally, she had an air of generous self-confidence I had not seen in any other adult.

Most of the self-confident adults I knew also carried with them a bit of defiance, perhaps an outcropping of self-defense. It seemed they were always on their guard. That if they stated a fact, someone was bound to dispute it. Or if they accomplished a feat, someone would attempt to find a flaw in it.

This self-protection was also contagious. I was already self-deprecating. I could not graciously accept compliments about my singing, piano playing, cheerleading, or appearance. My response to praise was inevitably a shy giggle and a quiet "Thank you," while thinking, "They're just saying that to be nice." Now, with all these new restrictions to my usually active life, coupled with the depression caused by the prednisone, I thought even less of myself.

In addition to English and algebra, I needed to complete studies in geography, social studies and science in order to stay on track. Administrators and teachers of the school were doing everything they could to assure that I would advance with my classmates to the next grade level.

I knew Mr. Nolan, because as a junior high cheerleader, I had watched him as he coached junior high football. A big, burly man with laughing dark eyes and a kind spirit, he exuded positive energy and plenty of it. At school, he taught social studies and US history. In accord with my eighth-grade curriculum, he was assigned to tutor me in geography and science.

I began looking forward to these one-on-one sessions with Mrs. Newell and Mr. Nolan. School work and studying took on a whole new meaning. It was interesting to see these educated teachers interact with my mother and siblings in the comfort of our home. They seemed more like real people here than at school.

My tutors were sensitive to my limitations in stamina. Sessions never lasted more than an hour and a half. Not only did they discuss subject matter with me, they taught me study techniques. Before reading a chapter, lesson, or test, they suggested I get an overview by reading the first paragraph or question and the last. This was to give me an idea of where I was going with my study, what I must accomplish. I became a much better student.

Perhaps like you, I only wished I could read the first and last chapters of my life. How was this dream to end?

CHAPTER 17

Altered Self

After an entire month living in my bed in the living room, the morning came when I would walk outside again. There was an appointment with the doctors at the hospital. I awoke, anxious to take my medicine, be bathed, and put on a real dress. Mother presented me with a new purple-checked seersucker dress with three-quarter length sleeves and an empire waist. I felt like a princess in the crisp loose-fitting garment.

I knew that Mother was pleased that I was smiling and comfortable and that she hoped the day would end as happily as it was beginning.

Walking out the back door was a strange sensation. Just carrying my body was something I had never before been so conscious of. The April air was cool and clean against my skin. I breathed deeply the scent of new growth releasing sweet odors through sleepy winter rot.

I was thrilled with the sensation of sitting in the car, the roar rushing under me, as bright tulips and sunny yellow daffodils slipped by.

Mother periodically asked me, "How are you feeling? Are you okay?"

Sometimes I answered, "I'm a little bit dizzy," or "It feels funny to go up these steps," but I added each time, "But I'll be fine. I'm okay."

Although the purpose of our venture was to see the doctors at the hospital and have my blood drawn, that was the low part of the day.

At the hospital, Mother and I found our way, first to the hematology lab where my blood was drawn, then to a little alcove of examination rooms and offices nearby. After we had waited briefly in an adjacent lounge, a cheerful nurse escorted us into a wood-paneled office.

She instructed me to step up onto a scale. The indisposed cheerleader's heart in me sank when the counterweight was pushed further and further to the right. One-twenty-five, one-thirty-two, 145 and a half! How could this be? I felt no different inside. How did this fat person take over my body? Just a month ago, when I was admitted to the hospital, I weighed 107 pounds! No wonder Mother had gotten this loose-fitting dress for me. True, empire waists were in style. But they were also convenient for fat people!

I would have to tell Carolyn in my next letter that the weight-losing contest was over. I wouldn't tell her why. That was too embarrassing. I would just say that, due to my illness, I would have to postpone the contest.

"Okay. You can step down now," the nurse instructed as she jotted on a clipboard. "Just have a seat here." She then took my temperature and blood pressure and felt my pulse.

"It will be just a few minutes." She smiled and left Mother and me alone in the unfamiliar room which smelled faintly of stale cigar smoke.

Soon, Dr. Knoch, the internist, and Dr. McKeon, the pathologist, entered the office. They alternately interrogated me. "Are you eating well?" "How is your appetite?" "Are you having difficulty going to the bathroom?" "What color are your bowel movements?" "Is your urine dark?"

I answered the last two questions by looking around the room at the subtle mottling of browns and tans in the wood paneling. I chose a patch for each and said, "I guess something like this."

Actually, I had never thought it important, much less desirable, to examine what I left in the toilet. Before hospitalization, my bowel movements were very light. By now, they were caramel brown. The urine was not bright yellow, but at least not quite as syrupy brown as previously.

Dr. McKeon explained, "What you excrete is a measure of how well your digestive tract is functioning."

It wasn't really something I wanted to dwell on, so I dismissed it quickly.

"Hop up on this table, young lady," Dr. Knoch ordered.

Obeying him, I laid back on the examining table. Dr. Knoch pulled a sheet up over my legs as he lifted my dress just to the breast line. Then he pressed first on my right side and asked me to take a deep breath. He repeated the procedure several times all over my abdomen. Next, he listened with his stethoscope as he instructed me to breathe deeply or normally.

"Okay. You can get down now," he finally said.

"So when can I go back to school?" I asked pointedly.

Dr. Knoch's teeny eyes squinted even further shut as he laughed. "Oh, you're not ready for that yet. A few more weeks of bed rest, and we'll see you again in a month."

"Will you let us know the results of her blood tests?" asked Mother. "Or should I call you to find out?"

"We will phone you in a few days," replied Dr. McKeon. "If you don't hear from us for some reason, you are welcome to call here."

As we drove from the hospital parking lot, Mother sensed that I was feeling gloomy.

"We'll just wait and see what those blood tests reveal," she said optimistically. "I'll bet you surprise them all!"

I continued to gaze blankly through the window, my chin cupped in my hand, my elbow propped on the armrest of the door. Mother suggested, "How about we stop at the Dairy Queen for a treat? Do you feel up to it?"

I loved ice cream. I was not anxious to return home and crawl back into bed.

"Oh, yes! That would be fun!"

It was nearly three o'clock in the afternoon when the car pulled into the driveway at home.

"Thank you, Mommy, I had a lot of fun being out today."

Together, we walked across the footbridge to the house. Mother climbed the long flight of steps by the side of the house behind me to be sure she could catch me if I stumbled.

Surely, she thought, my daughter must be tired after this long day of activity.

"May I wear my dress until bedtime?" I asked as I sat on the edge of the bed. "I'm kind of tired of wearing pajamas all the time."

"I think that would be just fine, darling," Mother answered with a smile. "You did very well today. But now, you must rest. I'll get supper."

A battle raged inside of me. I wanted to be someone even if I was restricted from participating in school and church events—restrictions from the routine activities of simply walking around or sleeping in my own upstairs bedroom. The battle raged with the dysfunction of my body, which was the whole reason for those restrictions.

Suddenly, there was the appearance of a body on the outside with a girl inside screaming, "Let me out of here. My spirit does not fit this body. I am someone different than the shell you see out there."

I laid myself back onto my bed and picked up my journal. There was a lot to process, and I was finding that writing to *Kim* was great therapy.

In addition to my journaling, I turned more and more to my Bible for comfort and guidance.

After all, I thought, God is the only one who can heal me. Surely I can influence his plan with my devotion to him. Only with God's help will I ever be able to live my life whatever it may be.

CHAPTER 18

Miracle Worker

I f you have ever contracted a cold or gotten a splinter or sprained an ankle or a wrist, and someone has found out about it, no doubt you've been offered advice. Your friends, relatives, neighbors, coworkers, even strangers have an opinion of what may help you heal.

Your Aunt Sara insists you need chicken broth as hot as you can bear for your cold. A splinter, according to your best friend, requires a tweezers for removal and an antibiotic ointment to prevent infection. Anyone on the block will tell you to ice your sprained ankle.

Then, if you suffer something more serious or more uncommon than a cold, just mention it in conversation, and suddenly, you hear every experience about a similar ailment ever suffered by anyone in the room. Females are especially familiar with this phenomenon. At age twelve when they have their first menstrual period, every female in the family over age twelve, even aunts they never spoke with before, tell the girl, "Oh, now you'll know what backache is all about!" "Aspirin may help those cramps a little bit." "A heating pad is your best friend." "Rest, rest, rest." "Stay as active as you can!"

Then, when a woman becomes pregnant for the first time, she hears every story any woman ever went through.

"With my first baby, I was so uncomfortable." "By the time you have your third, it will seem a breeze!" "Be sure you get an epidural and drugs, drugs are essential!" "It may hurt, but go natural. You'll forget the pain as soon as you see that beautiful little miracle." And on and on.

Even a case of tonsil removal will have sages on the subject emerging from the woodwork. The patient will hear about everything from the most primitive forms of surgery to the post-surgical joys of frozen confections.

Since my liver disorder was so rare and my prognosis so bleak, my desperate parents were bombarded with every home remedy and lay medical suggestion that ever entered the highly German population which surrounded them. The doctors prescribed eighty milligrams of prednisone per day, two eggs daily, a half-pound of meat per day, and as many carbohydrates as I could ingest in a day. In addition to this prescribed, already high protein regimen, I was to drink a twelve-ounce serving of Meritene, a protein-concentrated mix, twice a day.

Daddy had served in the Army Air Force in World War II. Several of his friends had either contracted hepatitis themselves or knew someone who had suffered briefly from the disorder while serving. This wasn't surprising as they lived in such close quarters, often shared a canteen of water, and were sometimes in unclean, disease-ridden environments overseas. Their major remembrance of treatment was hard candy. It supplied an immediate release of carbohydrates. As a result, Daddy provided a jar of sour balls near my bed. He made sure it was never empty.

An acquaintance of my mother's, who was the mother of seven children, swore by a tablespoonful of mineral oil each day mixed into a glass of grape juice for general health and as a cure-all. I consumed lots of mineral oil in grape juice in those early days of my illness. Supposedly, the grape juice was to mask the unpleasant feel and taste of the oil. It did not. The drink tasted like good grape juice contaminated with mineral oil. But I drank it obediently. Anything to get better so I could go back to school.

Some proclaimed that a few sessions with a chiropractor would heal me. Since the doctors had forbidden ventures from the house except for monthly visits to the hospital, I did not see the chiropractor in those first six months.

Then, Mrs. Markel, an elderly lady Mother and Daddy knew from church, suggested a woman who would visit me in our home. She was no chiropractor. She claimed no fancy modern medical education. This plump little lady, who wore her grey hair pulled tightly back in a neat little bun, practiced old German pow-wow.

Treva was willing to try almost anything to restore health to her thirteen-year-old daughter—anything to keep her from dying. She felt that God had presented this possibility before her. How could she deny her child a possible miracle?

It was an encounter I would remember long into my adult life.

I had been confined to my bed in the living room for forty-five days. Except for the day I had visited the hospital for blood tests and doctor's examinations, I had lived in pajamas. My days consisted of medications, meals, Meritene, and basin baths. I spent my time reading, writing in my journal, and watching some TV.

So when one day, the strange little lady, in her flowered cobbler apron and wire-rimmed glasses, came through the back door with Mother, escape was not an option. Initial introductions were made.

"Peggy, this is Mrs. McClure," Mother said politely as she helped the old lady off with her sweater. "Mrs. McClure, my daughter, Peggy."

I smiled briefly. In the awkward silence that followed, I noticed a distinctive odor of sweet hay and fried food coming from the woman.

"What can I do to help?" Mother offered.

"Heat about a cup of bacon fat," answered Mrs. McClure.

I pulled the covers up around my neck. My mother had told me this morning that this lady was coming. Maybe God could use her to help me get well. Mrs. Markel had recommended her as a very effective pow-wow lady. This was a brand-new experience for Mother as well, but she was sure it could do me no harm.

I wasn't so sure. As the bacon grease melted, the whole house started to smell like the old lady. Was she a witch? What would she ask for next? Eye of newt? Toenail of frog?

Mrs. McClure gently pulled the covers down from my neck and asked me to unbutton my pajama top. Taking the little saucepan of grease from Mother, she stood over me as I lay in my bed and asked, "Do you believe in Almighty God?"

"Yes," I squeaked. What else would I say? This little woman was in control.

At that, Mrs. McClure laid aside my pajama blouse, exposing my swollen abdomen. She began chanting some sing-song words that sounded like an unintelligible language. At the same time, she made motions with her hands over my head, neck, and abdomen. Still chanting, she gently poured the very warm, nearly hot, grease onto my abdomen. Then she rubbed it all over my belly as she said, "Do you believe in God Almighty?"

"Yes."

"And in his son, Jesus of Nazareth?"

"Yes."

Then, more chanting as she waved her hands all around and over my ailing body. The entire rite may have taken fifteen minutes. To me, it seemed like two hours. Reminiscent of my hospital classroom experience, my inner voice was my only comfort.

"Whatever you want, God," I prayed. "Help me to be open to your strength and love." I repeated this mantra over and over while the pow-wow lady greased me in bacon fat and chanted the magic words.

When she finished, Mrs. McClure closed my pajamas over my oiled abdomen. "We'll just let all this soak in." She smiled.

I replied weakly, "Okay. Thank you."

I did not want to deny God the possibility of using even this strange and somewhat scary ritual for healing.

A few weeks later, my bloodwork showed a marked improvement. Mother seemed to want to believe the pow-wow had a great deal to do with this. So she arranged three more visits with the woman, two in Mrs. McClure's own home.

Each time, I was a bit frightened. Why was this woman so mysterious? Isn't it possible she might be an agent of Satan? Is it possible to cloak black magic with words like "God" and "Jesus Christ"? On the other hand, I wasn't getting sicker.

The old lady seemed coated with grease. Her hair, pulled back tightly in a little knot against her neck, was white with hints of yellow. It reminded me of a once crisp white sheet of letter-writing paper, now aged and yellowed at the edges, still usable but no longer fresh and new.

This lady might have peeked out of the gingerbread house in Hansel and Gretel. Her moldy image coupled with her eerie chants and rituals placed her in the same mysterious guise as the three hags who open the story of Macbeth. Their prophecies were completely accurate. They somehow knew what would happen in the future. In a similar way, perhaps Mrs. McClure had a connection to the source of healing.

I was not in control of what was happening to my body. I had not chosen this illness. I could not make it go away with the blink of an eye. I had learned that there are workings in this life outside my little sphere of influence. And so, I must give God reign to use whomever and whatever he chose as a channel of his healing power.

My contact with the pow-wow lady was only the first of many incidents where I would step back and say inwardly, "Please, God, help me to be open to your many mysterious ways, your wonders to perform!"

CHAPTER 19

Questionable Hope

Monday, April 27, 1964

Dear Kim,

I just have to write.

How is it we become? Become what we are today from what we were yesterday and the day before yesterday and the day before that and on and on?

I was second born. First, there was a boy, my brother Richard. Two and a half years later, I was born. A girl, Kathryn, was born exactly two years after that, on my second birthday. Finally, when I was eight years old, little brother Timothy came along.

As the older girl, I was charged with looking after little sister Kathy from the first day she came home from the hospital with Mommy. I loved taking care of this little dark haired baby in my two-year-old world. We not only shared our birthday, but we shared a bedroom until I went to the hospital last month.

I cannot remember childhood without feeling my sister's tiny hand in my own. Constant playmates and confidantes, even as preschoolers, we did everything together. If an aunt or neighbor offered me a cookie, I asked for one for Kathy also.

One of my very earliest memories was when we walked down the block to the corner of the tree-lined city street to Vacation Bible School. This was a daily morning school at the huge stone church eight houses from ours on the same side of the street. Sessions were held for two weeks in the summer when school children were on summer vacation. At ages three and five, Kathy and I were not on vacation, but Mommy and Daddy thought we would have fun in summer Bible School.

On that sunny day in June, Kathy and I walked hand in hand to the big stone church. When we arrived inside, I was herded away with the other five-year-olds to one classroom, and Kathy was corralled into a different room with two- and three-year olds.

Very little time passed before one of my teachers escorted me out into the dark hallway where Kathy stood with one of her teachers, crying her little heart out. She ran to me, hugged my arm, and wept, "I want Mommy."

The grownups said I should walk Kathy home. Then, afterward, I could return to Bible School.

Obediently, we made the long walk home. Kathy's tears stopped when she realized she would see Mommy soon. Mommy understood that Kathy was young and very shy. She commended me for acting so grown up and sent me back down the street to the church.

When I arrived, the lawn was empty of people. It was so quiet. I went to the big oaken door and pulled. It would not open. Had everyone else gone home, too? I pulled and pulled, but the big heavy door would not open. I became very upset. To this day, I do not know if my knocking on the big door was simply not heard or if Bible School had already ended and no one was in the church. In my five-year-old mind, I had been abandoned. How could they lock me out after I had obeyed them? I ran home in tears.

When I turned seven, I joined the Brownies, the little girls' segment of Girl Scouts of America. Mommy and Daddy felt this would also be a good social experience for Kathy when she was old enough to join. So again, I looked after my little sister, making sure she got materials for craft projects, sticking with her on bus trips to the Enchanted Forest and Roadside America.

When we were elementary school age, we walked from Mother's beauty shop to the grocery store together. I was the spokesperson and the money carrier. I made sure Kathy always got at least as much of anything that I got. If there wasn't enough for both of us, I still made sure my little sister got something.

Mommy regarded me as a responsible little nurturer. She allowed her girls our separate lives.

But Kathy and I were very close. Kathy depended upon her big sister, and I was comfortable and confident, for the most part, in looking after her.

Then in 1959 July, our little brother Tim came along. Within his first six months, Mother broke her wrist in a fall while roller skating. She was still Tim's mama, but I became Mother's hands. At age nine, I was busy changing diapers and dressing the new baby. I gave him baths and rocked him to sleep.

I often had to act like an adult. I was feeling a keen loss of childhood. I needed more attention. I found escape in the pampered heroine of fiction and imagination.

When little girls hear or read the story about Heidi, they imagine being the vibrant little girl who lives with her grandfather in the Swiss Alps. I, on the other hand, identified with Heidi's invalid cousin, Charlotte, who was confined to a wheelchair and very weak. After much cajoling from Heidi, Charlotte was permitted to spend time at grandfather's home, an Alpine goat farm, because Heidi believed her cousin would be strengthened by sunshine and fresh mountain air. The girls played together, making wildflower necklaces on the rich green grass near the herds *of sheep. In the end, Charlotte was enriched by the experience and a much healthier child by the time her father came to retrieve her. I didn't want to be the vibrant Heidi but the invalid cousin.*

By the time I reached age twelve, I was devouring books by Grace Livingston Hill. Her heroines were always weak or ill or shut off from mainstream society. They found solace in long evenings reading the Bible by the dim light of an inadequate fire in the hearth or a kerosene lamp.

In all of these stories, the heroine was rescued by a gentle, strong man. In Charlotte's case, her father, Heidi's uncle, came to fetch her home, her health greatly improved, although not perfect. Elizabeth Barrett's life of illness was cheered and encouraged by her writing and by visits from the romantic poet, Robert Browning. Grace Livingston Hill's heroines always found strength to overcome their obstacles with the help of a good-looking, well-mannered man.

In considering the pattern of my life, I am wondering if my imagination has been influential in my poor health. Is it because I read and enjoyed these stories that I thought I, too, must get sick? If I had read stories instead about Amelia Earhart or Eleanor Roosevelt, would my body have remained strong and healthy?

At least the fictional characters I admired conquered their problems in the end. There was a positive outcome in one way or another in each case.

I am learning it takes a great deal of courage to live.

I could not anticipate the medical and physical demons I had to confront when I was first admitted to the hospital. Will I experience in actuality events of a degree not even my fictional heroines experienced only on the page?

Will I find courage? Will I be brave enough to keep plowing forward?

Time will tell.

Love,
Peggy

Peggy and Kathy at Enchanted Forest, 1959

Tuesday, May 5, 1964

Dear Kim,

Alone. So terribly alone. Darkness and chill right into my bones. Nowhere to go. Nothing to do. Can't I just take too many pills? Oops! Now everything is black and quiet and still. No one is saying, "How are you today?" No voices cheering me on. "Hang in there!" How easy for others to chant these meaningless platitudes with no idea of the pain in my heart. My worthless heart in an unproductive shell I can't even recognize as my own. How did I get stuck in this room with no doors? No windows? No air?

I hate this room, no, I abhor it! I'm trapped in its ugliness with no means of escape.

Every now and again, I glimpse a ray of hope. Just endure for a little while longer. Things will change. Leaves will once more decorate the trees. The sun will warm you and the birds will sing. I dream of riding a bicycle, of dancing on the beach, of running through the wind. But when? Oh, when?

Every day is the same. I am awake before anyone else gets out of bed. Then, Mother and Daddy get up and go through the routine of packing lunches, making breakfast, and in Daddy's case, going off to work.

Two or three days a week, usually Thursday and Friday, Mother also leaves the house to go to her beauty shop in the nearby town of Glen Rock. On those days, Mother has arranged for the neighbor lady, Ivalee, to stay with me. Ivalee is a tiny woman who has practical nursing experience. After Mother leaves, Ivalee gives me my bath, then keeps me company, while she dusts furniture or washes windows and floors. At lunchtime, she fixes soup and a sandwich for me or whatever Mother has prepared ahead of time. Her soft Southern drawl makes the day seem easy as she smiles and goes about her busyness.

Still, the days crawl by. I read Catherine Marshall's account of her husband, A Man Called Peter. I write a letter to my cousin at college; I watch a new TV game show called Jeopardy. How apropos. Jeopardy. That's what I'm in. I jeopardize my life if I leave this bed. I jeopardize my spirit by staying in it.

I'll read my Bible. Surely, if God has laid this burden upon me, He has also provided a way to cope. A reason to press on. Oh, where is the meaning? Is it not for me to know? Does God take pleasure in seeing if we can work it out? Is that His game? His recreation? His entertainment?

Will I ever leave this room again?

Love,
Peggy

CHAPTER 20

Fresh Air and Pain

While lying in my bed, I made a chain of colored paper links—pink, red, green, yellow, blue—each link representing another day. When the chain had the number of links equaling the number of days until my next doctor visit, I hung it on the woodwork of the window frame beside the bed with a little piece of Scotch tape. Every morning, first thing after waking up, I tore off a link. With each link I removed, I knew I was another day closer to walking outside into the fresh air for a trip to the hospital. I was convinced that, surely, since I was obeying all the rules, I would be declared healed when I next saw the doctors. I compliantly stayed in bed all the time except to walk across the room to my jerry-rigged closet bathroom and to walk to the kitchen sink where Mother gave me a sponge bath in the morning. Another link ripped away. I ate all the food placed before me, which was much more than I really wanted. Two more links gone. I took my pills and drank the gruesome Meritene shake twice a day. Soon, five more links were torn from the chain. The only thing that motivated me to endure all of this was the belief and hope that, by the next monthly doctor visit, I would be completely well and could resume my normal active lifestyle.

With each passing day, the paper chain grew shorter. The hospital visit came and went. I found myself still confined to bed. I made another paper chain to watch another month go by, keeping the same hope that soon I could ride bike and play volleyball and return to school.

Apparently, the doctors were simply pleased and slightly amazed that I continued to survive. My blood work had improved. The bilirubin level had decreased. I was no longer jaundiced and my overall digestive system was functioning better than before hospitalization. Medically, the prednisone was controlling further inflammation of the liver. Although both the liver and the spleen were still very enlarged, I was not in pain.

Remaining inactive for months, on a high protein/high carbohydrate diet, and taking eighty milligrams of prednisone daily, I was gaining weight. I did not know that a great deal of the weight resulted from fluid retention caused by the prednisone. I just felt fat. And very sad. I wanted to scream, "This is not me you are looking at. I am an active, trim girl. Not a fat lazy slob." Mother was quick to tell me that people said I was still a very pretty girl, but I was sure they just pitied me. "What else would they say about a kid who was so sick?" I uttered this only in my own mind. I could not let anyone know how angry, confused, and upset I was because my life was turned upside-down.

Another month passed. It was June 1964. School was closing. Even though I had studied at home from my sickbed, my final grades demonstrated that I had passed to ninth grade.

Last year at this time, I would have been mailing out invitations for my first swimming party of the summer. I would plan for boys who liked certain girls to be here at our country property and girls who liked certain boys to be here. I was a regular matchmaker. Of course, I would invite my favorite to be here also, imagining a beautiful, blue sky day and loads of fun. Mother would help me prepare sandwiches and snacks. The day would end with wistful goodbyes and lifelong memories of young romance. No sooner would everyone leave than I would be planning the next summer fun party.

But not this year.

The colorful paper chain on the window woodwork finally came down to the last link. On that day in June, Mother and I visited the hospital, where the lab techs drew blood, and Dr. McKeon and Dr. Knoch punched my gut.

The trip home was much brighter. The doctors said that I was now permitted to get outside a bit. I could walk several feet beyond my usual jaunts across the room to the bathroom. Mother suggested perhaps I could sit on a lawn lounger on the front porch. The doctors agreed to that, saying the fresh air might do me good.

Mother and I celebrated with a stop at the discount department store for rubber sandals and another stop for an ice cream treat. All the while, I fantasized about being able to ride bike before summer's end.

That June, I reclined on the lounger on the front porch and watched as Daddy painted the porch ceiling. It was glorious being out-side for hours, seeing the birds fly from tree to bush to tree again. I could watch my brother and sister splash in the pool. I heard them com-plain about the chores they were assigned. I would have done anything to be able to get up and help them pick the string beans and sweep the porches and sidewalk and bridges. But for now, I was just happy to be alive and breathing the fresh summer air. Daddy and Mother were hap-pier, too. When I asked if Daddy might place the lounger down in the side yard, I saw them flash smiles at each other.

"It's really not that much farther than the porch," I pleaded. "I just want to sit on the grass."

Mother looked at Daddy. "Maybe after we see the doctors in July, we can ask what they think. There is the long flight of steps alongside the house to negotiate before you get to the lawn, you know. Let's wait just another week to see what they say."

When the July appointment came, the doctors gave their approval, and I began spending entire afternoons on the lawn beside the house. I loved looking up at the canopy of lacy leaves in the stately black wal-nut tree. Mother planted brilliant impatiens and red and yellow coleus around its base. The sweet scent of summer grasses and country fresh air pelted my nostrils. The sun caressed my arms like a long missed friend. Life was getting better.

Then, one day, as I sat in my chair, reading and listening to the gurgling brook flowing under the bridge, a motorcycle buzzed into the driveway. My heart raced.

I had not seen Richard F. since before I was admitted to the hospital three months earlier. He greeted my father who was working on the car in the pavilion, then walked across the footbridge and squatted onto the ground beside my chair.

The visit was brief. And that was good. Although I loved seeing him and hearing his voice, I found I had little to say. What did my life consist of but reading, writing in my journal, and taking medicine? I couldn't talk about the deer I had seen on my last bike ride through the hollow or the progress I was making in swimming lengths in the pool. There was nothing to anticipate—no roller skating, no hikes, no youth retreats.

There were long, awkward silences. I almost wished he hadn't come. Now, I knew my life would never be the same. I was actually glad when he said he had to be on his way. As he revved up his bike and rode off down the road, my heart imploded.

CHAPTER 21

Hopelessness

Friday, August 28, 1964

Dear Kim,

Today is the anniversary of Dr. Martin Luther King, Jr.'s speech at the Lincoln Memorial. I remember seeing on the television a huge crowd of people, Negro and white people, together, listening as he repeated again and again, "I have a dream..." that all people will be free.

It sure doesn't look like that on the evening news. People being beaten with clubs by policemen. Or being sprayed with a hard stream of water from fire hoses.

God, what is the right thing to do? Should people make such a fuss or just accept the way things are? It isn't right that some people should be treated badly because they have a different skin color. But isn't there a better way to change things? Can things change?

Oh, sometimes I am just so sad. I don't think I'll ever be able to make a difference in this world. Maybe if I can be a missionary. I may as well. I'm never going to make the Olympics or even get married or anything I always dreamed about.

At least, if I'm a missionary, I can serve God and help other people. Maybe that's why I've gotten sick.

Oh, I just hate my life. I'm so confused. I hope God forgives me for being such a negative person. I know I should just be thankful I'm alive.

The doctors even say I can go back to school. I'm so afraid. I haven't done much of anything for an eternity.

Oh, well. Day by day.

Love,
Peggy

CHAPTER 22

Preparation

B y mid-August that year, I was permitted to take short walks, down the side stairs outside, over the bridge, and a few more yards over the gravel driveway to the road in front of the house. I was practicing for September when I would return to school on the school bus.

In years past, my siblings and I had always walked quite a distance to the bus stop. In my first year of school, it was a great adventure to walk down the road and around the bend. After turning the corner, brother Richard and I walked past a steep embankment, all the way watching squirrels and rabbits and birds busy at their everyday chores. The road was dirt in those days. So on wintry mornings, it was great fun as we skated over ice-covered potholes or stomped on them crunching their thin glaze. Finally, we would arrive in front of the old clapboard schoolhouse-turned-home for the poor boys who always smelled of wood smoke. In the mornings, we all played together until the bus came rattling down the road to us. After we boarded, the bus driver had to maneuver a turn-around in the narrow pull off beside the road.

In the afternoons, we were dropped off after the bus made the turn-around. Instead of retracing our morning walk back home up the road, Richard took me through the meadow grasses down the stream bank. There, we would have to cross the fast moving brook. Richard must have been a patient little boy, because many times, he had to wait as I hesitated with great anxiety as I thought about stepping onto one rock and then another. I was positive I would slip into the icy water and ruin my school shoes. Big brother Rich coaxed and coaxed, "Come on, Peggy. Don't be such a 'fraidy cat. You can do it."

Finally, I stepped out oh so carefully and made successful steps from rock to rock and then the final leap across the sparkling water to the opposite bank. What a great feeling to have hurdled this obstacle. I never would have tried if not for Rich's incessant encouragement. The rest of the walk home was a saunter through the fallow cornfield to Daddy's strawberry patch. Then up through the lush emerald grass by the spring, over the picnic grounds, and back across the bridge to the house.

When I advanced to second grade, the bus made its turn-around at the bend. Brother and sister no longer walked the final stretch to the schoolhouse. Instead, the wood smoke boys had to walk up that part of the road to meet the bus. Also, my brother and I no longer took the meadow shortcut. The walk up the stretch of road back to our house was not nearly as adventure packed as our stream-hopping days.

And now, seven years later and a lifetime of change away from those carefree days, I was entering ninth grade. Younger sister Kathy and me, her disease-stricken companion, had only to walk across the bridge and out to the road to get the bus. Richard was driving a car or his motorcycle to school. While attending school, I never knew why the route had changed. Later I learned, it was so that I could walk the least distance for the ride to school. My illness was the reason for the altered bus route.

A DREAM

Where am I going? I must get there soon. But where? What am I to do or bring? What is my mission? I am on the road, walking briskly.

There are others who seem comfortable here. They chat among themselves, meaningless banter, relaxed, at ease with their journey. This makes me even more uncomfortable. It seems I should know what's going on, but I have no idea. Maybe if I just join in and pretend that I know what's going on, I will find out where we are headed.

And so I try to speak with some of these others. But I am ignored. It is as if I do not exist. Or if they do see and hear me, they prefer not to recognize my presence. I am excluded, invisible, pointless.

Looking ahead, the road just stretches on. I encounter some rough terrain. A steep embankment to my right and a plunging embankment to my left. Stones and uneven ground make footing difficult. I must concentrate as much on looking where I will place my next step as gazing forward to see my destination.

Then, suddenly, I trip and begin to fall over the edge. I know I will be torn by branches and brush and I'll knock my skull wide open on some sharp rock.

And I awaken.

CHAPTER 23

The New Girl

September 2, 1964

Dear Kim,

You'd think the first day of school would be fun and exciting. Not so. I couldn't wait for it to end.

First of all, it felt so peculiar to ride on the bus again. Just the rolling and jolting, the starting and stopping. Made me feel half sick to my stomach.

Finally, we pulled up to the school. I had to walk way across the parking lot just to get into the building. It seemed so very far to go. Then, after making my way down the long hallway, I had to pull myself upstairs to my homeroom.

And that was all without books! What am I going to do when I have to carry books from class to class and home and back again?

As if that wasn't enough, at lunchtime, I was at my locker putting some books away and getting another notebook for the afternoon. Carolyn's locker is just two away from mine. They are in alphabetical order. Anyway, she was at her locker when I was at mine. She looked at me and said, "Peggy, is that you? I didn't recognize you. You've gained so much weight!"

I didn't know what to say, so I just said, "Yes. It's me." She smiled and laughed her silly little giggle, and hurried off to her next class or to be with her friends or something…maybe just to get away from me.

I feel like I don't even know how to carry on a conversation anymore. I've been alone for so long at home. I mean, I haven't been out doing things with friends so I can't talk about plans and what we did last week. And I really don't do anything exciting. Just take pills and read and try to keep on going.

Mother packs my lunch so that I get the right foods. All the kids who buy the school lunch must sit on one side of the cafeteria, filling in each seat at the long tables, tray to tray. There are a few tables on the other side of the room for those who carry their lunch. We can sit anywhere we like. I found a spot alone and began to unpack my sandwich. Jeanne O. came to me and said, "May I sit with you to eat?"

Of course, I welcomed her. She is very nice. Very smart too. We talked easily together. She asked me what I liked to read and what kind of music I listen to. Who knows? Maybe we can sit together again tomorrow.

It's very scary. I feel like I'm the same person I was before all this sickness began and I had to miss school, but everyone sees me as different.

Really, my life is a lot different. I get up early to read my Bible, looking for guidance from God. Surely, this is a path he has worked out for me, his purpose for my life.

I guess it just means that life will never be the same as it was before I went to the hospital.

I'm just glad you are here, Kim, to listen to me complain and cry.

Love,
Peggy

CHAPTER 24

Self-Loathing

As the weeks passed, I found my niche in the new world I was encountering. My classmates began to accept the fatter Peggy. I immersed myself in studying and studying well. Instead of going to cheerleading practice or to try out for the volleyball team, I became a scholarly spectator. Teachers began to expect the highest grade achievements from me.

However comfortable I may have appeared to be, inside, I was in turmoil. My spirit had not changed even though, now, instead of residing within a 110-pound body, it lived in a 155-pound body. I possessed three wraparound skirts, an aqua blue, a pale green, and a forest green on which I had fabric-painted a swath of daisies (an activity that kept me occupied while confined to bed). I had two empire-waist seersucker dresses. These clothes I carefully plotted to alternate throughout each week so it wouldn't be so apparent I was wearing the same thing again and again. As a young girl, my mother had sewn her school dresses from printed feedbags. I suppose I should have been happy that I had so many clothes to wear. Also, Mother and Daddy were working hard for every penny just to pay for my prescriptions, so a wardrobe of new clothes was out of the question.

Now at age fourteen, I generally wore knee-high socks which made me feel a bit more stylish. The trend in the mid-sixties was ever shortening skirts, eventually ending up as miniskirts by the time I reached college, with knee-high socks or go-go boots. Girls did not wear slacks to school. Dresses were the required dress code. Some girls wore nylon stockings. And of course, dressier occasions like church or a banquet called for the bare leg look.

This was a problem for me. I never noticed just exactly when it began, but my legs had become discolored. Instead of normal, even flesh-colored skin, my legs had become mottled flesh and brown colors. In later years, I heard a doctor refer to this discoloration as *brownulation*. This sounded like a process for making brown sugar to me. No one ever explained exactly what caused the abnormality—perhaps the effects of the prednisone on the blood and tissues, perhaps poor circulation due to the liver disorder.

Whatever the reason, Mother again came to the rescue. She found a product actually called leg makeup. This disgusting substance came in a large tube, like an enlarged toothpaste tube. When the tube was squeezed, out came a thick brown paste, a shade of brown lighter than peanut butter. Mother taught me to spread this paste evenly over my legs until the uneven natural color was camouflaged. It did the trick. Of course, it was not waterproof so it couldn't be used for swimming. In fact, after an evening out, when I showered, it was amazing to see the brown water, like coming from rusting pipes, flow down my legs and out the drain.

More and more, I loathed my body. I bruised so easily, sometimes just from carrying my books. I had to be careful not to bump against a table or chair or I would end up with a large hematoma, a bruise that collected blood and made a lump and caused an extreme burning sensation for fifteen minutes or longer. When that happened, an application of ice helped reduce the swelling and disperse the bruise beneath the skin. Often, what began as a two-inch round black and blue mark would result in a swath of bruise over my entire thigh the next day. I was overweight for a person measuring five feet, three and a half inches tall. My face was very round with very rosy cheeks. I felt that I looked like a

Campbell's soup kid. This, I learned later, was referred to as *moonface*, one of the first side effects of taking prednisone.

So I retreated inside of myself.

I did a lot of praying and reading the Bible. I became active in the local evangelistic youth organization, Youth for Christ. Christianity seemed to fit what I was going through. The emphasis was on the spirit, rather than the body. The apostle Paul also loathed his body: I Corinthians 5:6, 7—"Therefore we are always confident and know that as long as we are at home in the body we are away from the Lord. For we live by faith, not by sight" (NIV). The gospel according to Matthew 6:25–33 (New American Standard Bible) stressed, "Do not be worried about your life, as to what you will eat or what you will drink; nor for your body, as to what you will put on. Is not life more than food, and the body more than clothing? Look at the birds of the air, that they do not sow, nor reap nor gather into barns, and yet your heavenly Father feeds them. Are you not worth much more than they? Seek the kingdom of God and then all the rest will come."

So I sought the kingdom as best I knew how. Every morning, I rose at five o'clock so that I could spend an hour reading the Bible and in quiet meditation and prayer. At 6 a.m., I finished whatever schoolwork I hadn't gotten to the night before. By 6:50 a.m., after slamming Meritene and pills, I was out the door, Bible on top of my schoolbooks, ready to face the cruel onslaughts of my high school experience.

Just when it seemed I was learning to accept my new life, something would happen to remind me that I was not normal. One summer, as I was babysitting my country neighbors over the hill, I had the first of what I eventually dubbed my leg accidents. The six-year-old boy was very active. When, at one point, I reprimanded him for running in the house, he kicked me in the shin. The pain was excruciating. If I had been alone, I am sure I would have wailed. When I grabbed my leg, there was blood all over my hand, already seeping through my slacks. The child knew something was terribly wrong. I firmly ordered both him and his four-year-old sister to their rooms and commanded, "Don't come out until I say so."

Then, I went to the bathroom to tend to my wound. When I removed my socks, I saw what looked like hamburger. I did not know how to treat this, so, after sopping up the initial blood, I phoned my mother who was working in her beauty shop ten miles away. Mother calmly suggested I wash it with hydrogen peroxide, put some merthiolate on it, and then apply a Band-Aid. Obediently, I hung up the phone and went back to the medicine cabinet to perform this first aid. But as I rested my foot on the toilet seat and was just about to pour the peroxide on the wound, I had misgivings. This was no little scratch to be covered with a Band-Aid. The top layer of flesh had been caught at a point toward the foot and pushed up, tearing a wider and wider path of skin in an accordion fashion until it made a triangle exposing underlayers of flesh I had never before seen.

So I phoned Mother again. After telling her what I was seeing, Mother said she would phone a nearby neighbor and ask her to take me to the doctor. The rest is a blur. I do not know what happened with the children. Perhaps, Mrs. Roberts, the neighbor who came to my rescue, took them first to the beauty shop to stay with Mother and then me to the doctor. I do remember the doctor had difficulty stitching the wound. The skin was so thin (another side effect of the prednisone), the stitches kept tearing away. He said my skin was paper thin. But he patched me up. I don't remember if he gave antibiotics to guard against infection. There may not have been much known about that sort of thing at the time. I was still able to walk. But in the days and weeks that followed, I learned a great deal about changing wound dressings, something that never would have been part of my life if not for the illness.

On another occasion, one icy morning, as I was making my way across the walkway to the bridge just outside our home, I slipped. I juggled books, a lunch bag, and an umbrella with a metal point. As I stumbled to gain my balance, the point of the umbrella caught my leg and made a small puncture. It hurt badly, and worse, it was another reminder that I was very fragile. I made my way back into the house, crying, "I'm not going to school today."

Daddy, just about to leave for work, scolded, "Now, you can't let a little thing like this keep you from going to school. Come on. We'll patch you up."

I cried quietly the entire time Daddy and Mother helped with cleaning and covering the wound. As I pulled on a clean pair of knee socks, I thought, It's not just school I don't want to attend. I want to drop out of life!

Another interruption came in July 1966. I was soon to turn sixteen. Since my case was so rare at the time, the doctors were interested in seeing the condition of the liver. The pathologist at the York Hospital, who had continued to oversee my remarkable case, suggested a liver biopsy. This required a three-day hospitalization. The biopsy was performed in the bed in a semi-private room. Although the liver itself cannot be anesthetized, the area around it is first injected with Novocain. After the area is made sterile, the doctor inserts a syringe large enough to withdraw a portion of the liver for further study. In this case, all the preliminaries were performed, but as the suction began, I heard the doctor say, "Forget it. There is too much bleeding. We must abort the procedure."

So I had suffered terror in anticipating the process, the fear I associated with staying in the hospital, and the pain of the procedure itself, all to no avail.

I wanted to trust God, to accept this life as a way to glorify him. But since my body was constantly an obstacle to overcome, I became very discouraged. Then, I would get angry and hate myself for being discouraged, considering my attitude as a lack of faith.

The summer after I graduated high school, another study was suggested. This was a bone marrow test. In examining the bone marrow, doctors were hoping to discover further effects of the liver disorder. As the doctor discussed the procedure with me and Mother, the attending nurse stated that she had had this test once upon a time.

"It is not fun, but I will be there with you the whole time."

This was not comforting to me.

The procedure was performed, and never in my life had I experienced such incredible discomfort. The marrow is drawn from the most accessible bone in the body, the breast bone or sternum. Local anesthesia is not effective and general anesthesia is not recommended for such a brief, minimally invasive procedure. So for fifteen minutes, as the nurse held my hand and whispered, "You're doing very well, just a little bit longer," over and over again, I felt like my heart was being sucked out of me. A better description might be that the very life was being sucked from me. Experiencing this made it understandable why, when some-one is grieving, they beat their chests. Therein resides what feels like one's very soul.

But I survived. As I recall, not much was learned from that test either, except that I was a very sick young lady. However, it seemed that I continued to amaze the doctors with my tenacious survival.

Neither of these tests were meant to advance healing of the liver disorder. They were performed to further enlighten doctors concerning the disease process taking place in this young body. I was a specimen.

It wasn't all positive attitude and "Oh, I'm doing just fine," in those years. A few months following the biopsy, after three years of tak-ing prednisone and still being restricted from much physical activity, I decided I was never going to get well. Why was I taking this medication with all its awful side effects? Why was I trying so hard to stay alive? I wasn't all that happy. I could not foresee a full life with college and work and marriage and children. Why bother taking this medicine?

When one takes prednisone for a period of time, the adrenal glands no longer produce cortisol, the natural hormone the body uses to protect us against illness and to cope with stress, part of the *flight or fight* phenomenon. The adrenal gland releases this hormone when we experience trauma to place us in a state of shock, so our bodies can deal with the ordeal at hand. Since the prednisone replaces that function, the adrenal gland becomes lazy. To terminate administration of the drug, it must be tapered very gradually so that the adrenal gland resumes its own activity. Otherwise, the body cannot guard itself from severe shock or even the trauma of a fever.

For some reason, perhaps because I was just a teenager, I was never informed of this.

So in my depression (yet another side effect of the drug), I just stopped taking the prednisone. I wanted to live like everyone else—get up in the morning, at the last minute if I wanted, throw on some clothes, and out the door. I wanted to not have to get out of bed early enough to take medicine, drink Meritene, and eat a healthy breakfast, even before gathering books to leave for school. But by this time, I was responsible for taking the medication without supervision from my parents. Every morning before school, usually just following breakfast,

I faithfully counted out my pills and swallowed them. I thought no one would ever know if I did not take the pills.

However, every two months, I was taken to the lab to get my blood tested. One day, after about four months of not taking the medication, the doctor called on the telephone and spoke with Mother.

"He is very alarmed. We have to go to see him right away," she told me when she hung up the phone. I wasn't feeling any more poorly than I had when I was taking the medicine. But I did feel a bit sick when I realized that he must know.

CHAPTER 25

Lecture

As I sat in a big uncomfortable wooden chair opposite Dr. Knoch's huge, polished, cherry wood desk, he almost disappeared on the other side. The more I got to know him, the more he took on the characteristics of a weasel in my mind. Now, as he was swallowed up by a much too big leather upholstered wing-backed chair, he looked like a little rodent peering out of his hole.

"Your blood levels have regressed significantly in the last month. Your enzyme levels are much too high and the bilirubin level is also elevated."

He paused to wait for my reaction. I gave him none.

"Why do you think this is? It seemed things were actually getting a bit better before this. You don't want to go back to the hospital, do you?"

More than a possible solution, it seemed like a threat.

I shifted in the chair.

"Well, I'm just tired of taking medicine and gaining weight," I confessed.

Perhaps, if Dr. Phil were sitting in that leather cushioned chair, I would have heard, "How does that make you feel? Having to take medicine and gaining weight?"

But Dr. Phil was probably about my age at the time, sixteen, so instead, I was stuck with Dr. Knoch and heard, "You can't just stop taking the medication…don't you know you're lucky to be alive, young lady?"

Sometimes, I didn't feel very lucky. My life just didn't seem to be what I expected.

This would have been a good time for him to explain to me that the side effects of prednisone include moderate to severe depression, water weight gain, and elevated blood sugar levels, among other unpleasant issues. Awareness often leads to self-understanding and self-forgiveness. Instead, he chose to warn me of other dangers I may get myself into because I wasn't a normal girl.

"Don't you ever get pregnant, young lady. The baby would kill you and your liver would kill the baby."

If he was trying to lift my spirits, he had chosen the wrong tack.

I suppose he spoke with Mother that day. But all I remember is a rough scolding. I thought of how badly my parents would feel if I died. And in spite of my ever-looming depression, there were days I did enjoy living.

This incident peaked my curiosity enough to send me to the library to do some of my own research. I learned that babies carried by mothers who take prednisone are often born with abnormalities—a water-logged brain, organs that are too large or too small.

I had always loved babysitting my little brother Tim. When we visited with younger cousins, my sister and I had fun entertaining them with pretending and running and playing. We loved looking after the children. We even thought of names we would give our own children someday.

Now, another of my dreams was crushed.

I dutifully went back to taking the medicine, although I wasn't sure exactly why. After all, what was there to live for?

Fun in the mountains, 1965

Spring 1967

Youth for Christ Spring Formal
1968

CHAPTER 26

Unforeseen Achievement

In high school, as I dealt with the effects of the disease and the drugs, I turned to God. I thought, If I could have faith enough, reach perfection enough, surely my body will be healed. Healed means I would have no more bad blood, my legs would return to their normal flesh color, my energy would be boundless, there would be no scars, no evidence of any illness!

So I clung to survival in the only way I knew how. I did what I could from day to day, what my energy and limitations allowed me to do. I grasped onto whatever rope was thrown to me—alternative treatments like mineral oil and pow-wow, dedicating myself to God and evangelism. I had no other choice.

This was a dream from which I could not wake up.

There were many good days at school. As I learned better study skills, I was able to participate in class when called upon. Instead of going to cheerleading practice and hanging out with the athletic teens, I made new friends. Jeanne, Bruce, Carol, and Beverly all enjoyed talking about what they were studying in chemistry, English, and trigonometry. They also did a lot of outside reading and integrated their knowledge of current events into the flow of the conversation. Just two years before, I never would have thought myself capable of holding my own with the likes of these scholarly types.

My high school years were 1965 through 1968, when young people flocked to Woodstock, and Newsweek headlined Haight-Ashbury. My best friend, Jeanne, was a musician who played the guitar and sang; she performed with her brother in a school assembly. They played and sang Simon and Garfunkel's newly released "The Sounds of Silence." Young minds were challenged every day with new and different ideas.

The Vietnam conflict was in full swing. Brother Richard was drafted into the army. We received a mimeographed letter with just his signature from Fort Hood, Texas, when he was in basic training. We missed him at Christmastime and wondered where he might be sent. He entered Officers Candidate School in Colorado Springs, where he lived off-base with a family who appreciated the arts. There, Richard was able to play the piano. On base, he coordinated a little acting group for entertaining the troops.

My faith in God and prayer and my activities with the church youth group and with Youth for Christ sustained me in those difficult years. As I moved from day to day, still taking large doses of prednisone, my life seemed very much a dream. Going to school. Having blood drawn for testing. Doctor visits. Taking medication. Singing in chorus, singing solos and in groups, and participating in Bible quizzes at Youth for Christ. I performed matronly roles in high school plays and practiced piano.

The leaders of Penn Mar Youth for Christ were Lamar and Ruth Carman. Their commitment to Christ and to young people was astounding. Outside of regular Saturday night meetings, Lamar and Ruth welcomed teenagers into their home. Many times, we sat around their dining room table chatting about books and politics and past experiences. They made me feel very much a part of the Youth for Christ family, but I always wondered how I could become as committed as they were. It seemed I could not hear God well enough to know his will for my life. That was a huge phrase in those days: *God's will for your life*. I'm not sure anyone really knew what that meant. Lamar and Ruth spoke of having met by accident, of how they filled the need for leadership at YFC when the former leader walked away. It seemed to me these things just happened, not by any choice or intense planning because God had told them to do it. I continued to puzzle over what might be God's will for my life.

Before long, I graduated, second in my class. This seemed so very honorable and amazing to many. "She must be smart!" was a frequent comment. But studying was my sole activity besides music, so to me, it didn't seem such an amazing accomplishment.

However, I did try to make it memorable for those I loved, for those who would be so proud. I didn't talk about it at home. They already knew I would be asked to make a speech in the graduation ceremony. But I didn't tell anyone that I was also going to sing (except, of course, those who were coordinating the evening's events).

In June of 1968, a few days following the assassination of Senator Robert Kennedy, two months following the assassination of Dr. Martin Luther King Jr., my classmates and I graduated. My friend Jeannie O. was valedictorian; I was salutatorian of our class of 126 students. Jeannie gave a wonderful scholarly speech befitting her achievement. My speech was very brief so that I had time to sing:

> "Let there be peace on earth,
> And let it begin with me..."

As the last strain of music floated into the June evening, there wasn't a dry eye within hearing range.

Perhaps this was why I was still alive. But would I ever find peace for myself?

High School Graduate
June 1968

CHAPTER 27

Necessary Farewells

Sunday, July 14, 1968

Dear Kim,

I have loved the gift you have given me of writing all my troubles, joys, and thoughts here, without judgment or advice. You have been a true and helpful friend.

However, I have found myself reading and rereading past entries, and I'm not so sure that is healthy, psychologically. Like maybe I have learned some lessons from those experiences and should not "go back" there again.

So now, I must bid you "goodbye" with thanks and a bit of sadness.

I will never forget you.

Love,
Peggy

After this writing, I carried my green paper notebook outside, down the steps, across the bridge, past the springhouse, to the burn barrel. There, where I performed the weekly chore of burning the trash, I placed *Kim*, lit a match, and touched the flame to the corner of that precious paper treasure. I watched as each page slowly caught fire and burned to ashes. I thought, *Never again will I revisit these awful memories. I need to find myself in some other way.*

After graduation from high school, I wanted to find a summer job. I had heard about a Christian summer camp in Maryland, not too far from Glen Rock. River Valley Ranch was established by the Bissett brothers, John and Paul, natives of Scotland, who had settled in the green hills of Maryland. To serve the Lord, the Bissetts aired a radio program in which they taught their very conservative Bible-based doctrine. They also broadcasted the job openings at RVR for young people with a Christian faith.

I interviewed for a position as *worker* and was assigned to the Junior Camp. My job entailed cleaning up bathrooms and showers used by kids ages twelve to fourteen. When I wasn't engaged in sweeping and scrubbing and swishing at the Junior Camp, I was house cleaning for an adult couple who were ranch workers. Betsy was six months' pregnant that summer. Bill was one of the horse wranglers as well as a weekend clown at the Saturday afternoon rodeos. They really appreciated my skill and dedication.

All RVR workers were required to attend the nightly evangelical services. These hour and a half long meetings included singing, lengthy prayer by John or Paul or one of their nephews or other resident ministers. Special music, a solo, duet, or trio, was always my favorite part of the service. Finally came the half-hour to forty-five-minute sermon, charging those in attendance with their sinful nature and dire need to ask Jesus to atone for them. More music, often the hymn "Just as I Am," ended the evening with the speaker beckoning unconverted sinners to walk forward to the altar to be saved.

When this final hymn began, a handful of workers unobtrusively exited the tent to staff the ice cream shop.

After campers were dismissed from the meeting, they flooded the ice cream shop, clamoring to buy their favorite frozen confection. As I scooped vanilla, chocolate marshmallow, and strawberry icy dairy cream into cones, I bumped elbows with one of my bunkmates, Alice. When there was a lull in the frenzy, as we wiped the counter and washed stickiness from our arms and hands, we chatted.

"Are you going to college in the fall, Peggy?" Alice was comfortable making conversation anywhere, anytime.

"I'm hoping to go to Wheaton College out near Chicago."

Sharing future plans was always risky for me. I wasn't sure I would survive this River Valley Ranch ordeal, much less enter college at summer's end.

"You're kidding me!" Alice almost bounded off the ice cream case. "I'm going there, too! We'll probably be in classes together!"

Alice was already a world traveler. Her home was in Silver Spring, Maryland, a suburb of Washington, DC. She had visited relatives in Indiana and in Sweden. So attending college in Wheaton, Illinois, was, for her, just a walk across the city square. For me, it was going to be a whole new world.

Compensation for our work cleaning up after adolescent campers, serving their meals, housecleaning, ironing, and scooping up sticky treats was a measly $4.50 per week. I surmised this was pre-missionary experience. More a privilege to work at a Christian camp than a summer job to earn tuition fees.

In the two-hour "free time" workers were granted from 2 p.m. to 4 p.m., Tuesday and Thursday, they could swim in the pool or ride a horse with other workers. I was extremely self-conscious of my brown splotched legs and my fat body. By this time, on the lower dose of prednisone, I had lost some of the water weight. As my activity had increased at school and at home, the weight dropped slowly from the 150s to the 140s. I was more and more aware that a person's appearance did not necessarily reflect their personality. A body is the home in which the spirit lives. Everyone's house is different, but can be welcoming. Still, I shied away from swim wear and opted to ride a horse.

I was not a very experienced rider, so the wrangler in charge chose one of the older, less frisky horses for me. He also placed me toward the end of the line of seven riders. Two were riding specialists, the others were ranch workers out for a pleasure ride. It was another hot late July day. I mounted "Smokey" with little assistance. As the group started ambling across the meadow, I felt relatively safe on my mild-mannered steed. However, the longer I sat on my moving perch, the more I became aware of pressure points to my thighs, knees, and buttocks. It felt like I was already bruising and I was barely ten minutes into the ride.

I reached the breaking point when I entered the woods. To scale the slight upslope, the horse needed to canter. Although the horse had walked this path many times before, I was totally unprepared for the increase in speed and the uneven gait. In my panic, I did not dodge tree branches and soon had scratches on my face and neck and a huge lump of fear in my chest. I felt I was going to slip off the horse.

The riding coordinator, Brad, was quick to recognize that I was completely out of control. Smokey sensed my panic and reacted by racing to the head of the line. Brad grabbed Smokey's reins and slowed the animal. He calmed me, saying, "It's okay. The horse had to canter to get up the hill."

"I'm sorry," I whimpered. "I never should have tried riding. I'd like to go back now."

So Brad's assistant guided the remainder of the ride, as he led me and Smokey back to the stables. Tears furrowing the dust on my cheeks, I quaked as I dismounted the gentle horse.

Brad patted my shoulder. "Really, it's okay. Next time will be better."

As far as I was concerned, there would never be a next time. I was bruised, exhausted, and had had more than enough of River Valley Ranch and missionary training. For me, it was just another message that I could not participate in life the way I would like.

After three weeks at River Valley Ranch, I returned home.

Later that summer, in August, my parents gave a birthday/going-away party for me. Memories of this joyous time have faded. It also seemed like a dream. I would be leaving for Wheaton College, Illinois, within the week. I had lived in the country outside the little town of Glen Rock for thirteen of my eighteen years. Now, I was about to travel to a mid-sized town twenty-five miles west of the great metropolis of Chicago, no small undertaking for a protected, sickly young woman.

I had hoped God would show me it was his will that I attend Wheaton. I applied to only this one college. I reasoned, if God didn't want me there, I wouldn't be accepted. However, it was no surprise that I was accepted as a student at Wheaton. I was an excellent student, earning straight As in all my school subjects; I had been very active in both my church youth group and in Youth for Christ; I performed well in my piano studies. I even considered applying to Wheaton's Conservatory of Music. My piano teacher, Mrs. Elsie Nelson, however, wisely advised that I first apply to the College and, after being accepted there, if I wanted, I could transfer to their Conservatory. Wheaton's motto is "For Christ and His Kingdom." Surely, God was directing me there.

None of this seemed real until the evening when I sat at my Wheaton College dorm room window looking down on the parking lot. My mother and father and little brother, Tim, were climbing into the Chevy in which we had traveled the long miles across Pennsylvania, into Ohio, through Indiana, and after eighteen hours on the road, arrived in Wheaton, Illinois, together. As they drove out of sight that warm September night, I realized I would not be with them again until Christmas. Maybe living apart from them would disturb me from this dream and I would awaken to reality.

DREAM

*T*he grass is soft under my feet as I run into the sunshine. A bird flies past me so closely, I could almost touch it. But too quickly it is gone. My joy is tentative as I tiptoe forth to see what wonders may come my way. In the distance, across the great expanse of green, I see a little girl on a swing. She does not glide back and forth, I hear no laughter. As I approach, she turns her face from me. She hugs her dolly and swipes her nose and then she runs away.

My joy is gone. I ache for the little girl. What has made her so sad on such a beautiful day?

And then I notice the sun has clouded over. The grass feels prickly like straw. The only birds I hear are the cawing crows that hulk on tree branches frightening other birds away.

Why am I here? Can't I go home? I have no joy. All I want is peace.

And I awaken.

CHAPTER 28

Lessons in Life and Love

One of my first evenings at Wheaton, all the girls in Smith Hall were summoned to the lobby for a dorm meeting. The resident assistants and house mother gave a program detailing the rules of the dorm: no men on floors or in rooms, just in the lobby when the dorm was open. Doors locked at ten p.m.; you had to be in by then. RAs would enforce noise levels and behavior on the floors.

Then a few upperclass women performed a skit, in which a single girl was walking back to the dorm from campus and a couple of guys attacked her. This was followed by the admonition that, although an incident like this is unlikely to happen, Wheaton is very accessible to Chicago by way of the train, so don't go out at night in groups of less than five or six.

This, to a country girl accustomed to taking long, lonely walks in the crisp woodsy air near my Pennsylvania home, was terrifying. The dorm was off campus by at least two city blocks and a very dimly lit roadway. My experience at college was certainly beginning with new possibilities!

In my World History class, the young man in the seat next to mine was a prince from a small African country. He was distinguished with a symmetrical pattern of scars all over his face. Certainly, this was something I had never before encountered. We were both presented with the same challenge when the professor announced that there would be a test on one of the textbooks at the end of the first week. I had never read an entire book in a week. Having excelled in high school, I was extremely upset that I couldn't complete this assignment. I cried myself to sleep more than one night that week. Why did I think I could ever get through college? It takes so much effort just to walk to the dining hall and to classes. When Friday arrived, I sat next to the prince in great fear of what was coming. The test turned out to be a multiple choice quiz of fifteen general questions. I answered all but one correctly.

Besides the intellectual provocation and inquiry, Wheaton classes presented a spiritual phenomenon, as well. In keeping with the college slogan *For Christ and His Kingdom*, every class began with devotions. Each professor was permitted their own interpretation of what comprised these few moments before the actual teaching began. The professor of World History followed a rather traditional pattern of reading a passage of scripture and then praying aloud for a few moments. The anthropology professor chose to read a passage from a variety of religious texts and then said a few words of blessing. The philosophy professor, a small oriental man, read sometimes from scripture, sometimes from poetry, sometimes from a philosophical extract, and then asked for a few moments of silence when students were encouraged to pray silently.

Students at Wheaton came from all over the United States and throughout the world. Some were children of missionaries stationed in the Far East or in Europe or Africa. Some were indigent students of those missionaries come to the US for further education. This geographical variety brought with it an expansive variety of thought and morals, all very new to me, the sheltered Pennsylvania student.

The little country girl from Glen Rock became friends with girls who hailed from Boulder, Colorado; Berkley, California; Rome, Italy; and Sidney, Australia. My roommate, Ruth, was a resident of Girard, northwestern Pennsylvania. Ruth was Plymouth Brethren by faith, a denomination I had never heard of. The women of this assembly were required to cover their heads for worship. So Ruth had a closet full of beautiful, chic forty-plus dollar hats. I was troubled by this, having read in the Bible that one was to "sell all that (we) have and give to the poor." My suitemates were from Boston, Massachusetts, and Kenosha, Wisconsin; my resident assistant was from Los Angeles; and my "big sister" was from Lancaster, Pennsylvania. I developed a close relationship with a girl who lived in nearby Oak Lawn, who invited me to her home for the long Thanksgiving weekend. I was sure I was regarded as that simple girl from the Amish country.

Pennsylvania winters provided enough snow for sledding and closed-school-days. But Wheaton winters were nasty, with temperatures consistently in the low 'teens and never ending winds from Lake Michigan, even though it was twenty-five miles to the East. Between the frigid temperatures and gusting winds, staying stylish for classes, much less comfortably warm, was nearly impossible. It was usual to step outside, and instantly, all the moisture in your nose would freeze.

I was excited about studying American Literature. I had always done very well in English studies. In fact, I scored high enough on my pre-college accelerated English exam that I was exempted from the regular freshman basic English course and placed in this Am Lit class instead. Writings that were part of the course included Jonathan Edwards' *Sinners in the Hands of an Angry God*, Herman Melville's *Moby Dick*, Nathaniel Hawthorne's *The Scarlet Letter*, and Thomas Paine's *Common Sense*. The professor was an unmarried devotee of all things letters and sped through lectures with great passion. The time came for the first exam, a mixture of multiple choice questions, and two essay questions. Although I had studied well, I was bewildered by some of the questions on the test. I did my best in the allotted time. A week later, when the professor returned the graded exams, I found I had scored a D! This was unacceptable! But as I read the corrected exam and observed the professor in subsequent lectures, I noticed that I should concentrate on what the prof emphasized in class. I busied my bright pink highlighter whenever the prof read a passage and commented on it. With such a massive amount of material covered, narrowing my focus in this way actually made studying much easier. The next exam came and went and I scored an A.

It was in this class I met a soft-spoken fellow from Pittsburgh. Greg had beautiful blue eyes, somewhat thinning hair, and was very tall.

As far as I knew, I never flirted with him, but was merely friendly when he said hello or discussed class material briefly before or after class.

Although I had abandoned *Kim*, I continued to journal. It seemed the only way for me to vent and stay sane.

February, 1969,
second semester freshman

I am so very confused—and sad—so sad. I know Christians are supposed to be full of joy and assured that God is guiding their every step.

But I have been pleading with God to guide me, to show me His will for my life. And I am sure of nothing.

How can I declare a major I'm sure of if I don't know what God wants me to do? I have heard so many people testify that God placed them in such and such a career or that God guided them to go to such and such a needy country to serve the people there. And although they have very little, certainly not all the comforts of the average American, they are happy serving the Lord and these people who need them.

I have sought and sought God's guidance. As far as a major goes, I can't even be sure I will live to graduate from college. How can I visualize myself in a career as teacher, missionary, or translator? I can't imagine living overseas far from my doctor and the medical sophistication of the USA. I don't even know if I could withstand all the vaccinations needed to travel to a foreign country. Are there contraindications to the medicine I now take that has kept me alive?

So I have declared Christian Education as my major. I thought that should be all-encompassing. It's a good base whether I serve as missionary or as Christian Education Director in a church.

I also love French. My fantasy is to go to France and teach there in a Christian setting. Or to be a translator somehow. But I can't really imagine that happening.

*Still, I have signed up for a linguistics class next semester.
We'll see where that leads.*

Peggy

April 1969

*Oh sigh. I feel so out of place. My roommate, Ruth, is
mooning over this guy who is a junior. I was so afraid to
go out with Greg that I actually told him I had to study for
a geology exam. I had been looking forward to attending
the Royal Shakespeare production of All's Well That Ends
Well. But then Greg asked if I would go with him and I
just blurted out the first excuse I could think of.*

*Last month, we had a dorm open house. All the girls
were welcome to invite a boy as their guest. I invited Greg.
Part of the evening was organized games in the dorm lobby.
We played a game called "Wink." All the guys sit in chairs
which are arranged in a circle. The girls sit on the guys'
laps, except one guy is without a girl. He winks at another
girl in the circle. The object is for her to "escape" her guy's
lap and run to the winker's lap. Her guy must "catch" her
before she escapes. He cannot get up out of the chair to pur-
sue her, he must latch onto her before she gets away. Well,
in my prudish mind, Greg was enjoying this game far too
much. I didn't know what may come next.*

*So once I told him I was going to study, I couldn't go to
the play. I would have been lying. And if Greg went anyway
and saw me there, he would have seen I had lied to him. So I
just stayed in the dorm and studied instead of seeing the show.*

*What is wrong with me? Greg is very nice. I am just
afraid of getting too close to anyone. I don't want to hurt their
feelings. And I don't want them to get to know me too well.*

I'm afraid they'll be disappointed.

I am.

Peggy

I completed my first year at Wheaton with a great sigh of relief. Spring came at last! A break from the bitter chill of Illinois winter! I traveled east to my Pennsylvania home in the woods with elation and with trepidation that somehow I had changed. Or at least, those at home would perceive that I had changed.

Truly, there had been changes in my thinking. I knew the world was much larger than my southern York County community. I knew there were many different ways to worship God. Wheaton had churches of every denomination in existence, or so it seemed. I had attended Plymouth Brethren, Pentecostal, Episcopalian, Presbyterian, and Catholic services. My classmates hailed from Africa, Asia, Australia, Spain, Sweden, Hawaii, and many other states. I had dated an African American man from Newark, New Jersey. I had attended symphony concerts, opera, and the ballet.

In many ways, I was not the same girl who left for college the September before. In many ways, I remained the frightened, insecure girl dealing with the uncertainties of illness.

When I returned to York County, I found a job as store clerk for the summer. I wrestled with whether or not I should return to Wheaton, so far away, where I felt so out of place. Alice had arranged that, as sophomores, we would share a room in Williston Hall, a much homier environment than the institutional, rubber-stamped Smith Hall where I lived my freshman year. We had both declared ourselves Christian Education majors, so we would be attending several of the same classes. I was now familiar with the campus and the routines of attending required chapel in the morning, tramping over the campus to classes, and spending hours in the library. Surely, I could return for my second year and become more secure and happy. I felt I just had to return to prove to myself that I could do it.

When September came, Mother and Daddy drove me over the long roads back to Wheaton. I arrived to learn that my close friend from Oak Lawn, Barb Gross, had withdrawn from the school. The year before, Barb and her family had welcomed me into their home like another daughter and sister on holidays and semester break. She promised to visit on campus, but I knew, as her life changed, I would become a memory.

Nevertheless, Alice and I made our room in Williston warm and welcoming. Alice occasionally worked for a catering service. On the nights she had a job, she often brought back boxes of leftover croissants, hors d'oeuvres and finger foods. College students, always famished, converged on our room and, with laughter and chatter, devoured every last crumb.

Still, I felt lonely and lost.

In Smith Hall the year before, I had lived in a suite, two rooms connected by a bathroom with shower, toilet, sink, and mirror. There was a modicum of privacy. In Williston, everyone on the floor shared a large bathroom, as might be in a locker room, with a row of showers and toilet stalls and another row of wash basins. This, of course, meant that, whenever I showered, my discolored legs were seen by anyone else in the bathroom at that time. Not only was I seen by others, but I saw, what appeared to me, their beautifully perfect bodies. Just another reminder that I was not normal.

November 1969,
first semester sophomore

Oh my! I can't wait to get back home for Christmas, even if it is for just a little over a week. I haven't been home since I got here in early September. I miss my little brother, my sister, my Mother and Daddy. I can't wait to cuddle the dog and cats. Just to sleep in my own bed will be a dream come true!

We'll bake cookies. I'll play our piano. I'll walk down our country road. I'll read letters from my big brother in the army.

And yet I'm scared too. Has college changed me? Will people treat me differently now that I've been away?

Oh, life is so uncertain.

But it's Advent. Surely the joy of the season and cele-brating Christ's birth can lift my spirits.

Peggy

December 16, 1969

I just don't understand. All I have learned tells me Christians are to "love one another as (Christ) has loved you." We talk all the time about helping the needy. Reaching out to those who are helpless or without hope.

And yet, last night, I was so very depressed...not knowing how to make plans for my life or even for the next year at school. I cannot imagine myself ever getting married and having a family. My health will prevent that. And yet here I am at this expensive college, spending my dear parents' hard-earned money, for what? So I can be better than them? I don't want to be better than them! I just want to be normal!

So I sat on the floor in Williston's dorm lobby in front of the beautifully lit Christmas tree. I cried and cried and cried, watching the multicolored lights turn into prisms through my tears. And, here, in the midst of this supposedly Christian college, not one person stopped to ask if they could help or get me a drink of water or what was wrong. That only adds to the sadness.

What a nightmare!

Peggy

In spite of my confusion and depression, I was a finisher. So I continued to do well in my studies—Introduction to New Testament, Geology, Christian Education of Children. But by the time I took my last final exam in January 1970, I was spent with homesickness and uncertainty of the future. I phoned home and Daddy answered, "Hello, princess."

"Daddy, I want to come home," I choked back the tears.

"You just tell us when you want us to come to get you," was all he said. He must have sensed my uncertainty and great longing for home.

I also had a heart-to-heart with God. Standing alone in our room in Williston Hall, I argued, "Lord, I have sought you in every way I know how. I have read the Bible, listened to those who speak on your behalf, and taken what they have said seriously. I have tried to fashion my life after yours. And still, I do not know what it is you want me to do!" Then, shaking my fist in the air, "So from here on out, you must find me. I am going to live as fully as I can, learn as much as I can, participate in life without fear of offending you. You have told me in your Word that you are the truth. I am going to seek the truth, so I should end up right back in your arms. But I am no longer going to call myself a Christian. If people find my actions to be Christ-like, fine. But I herewith release that label."

As tears blinded me, I packed up my few belongings. When Mother and Daddy arrived a couple days later, without even saying goodbye to Alice, I climbed into the car with my beautiful family and made one last trip from Illinois to Pennsylvania.

I left Wheaton, depressed, uncertain, and near suicidal. For two weeks, I remained in my room, occasionally coaxed out for a bite to eat and to take medicine.

When I piled my stuff into the car in Illinois that for that final ride home, I weighed 135 pounds. My clothes felt a bit more comfortable. I was beginning to resign myself to the fact that I would never have a Peggy Fleming figure-skating body. Did the weight difference alter my self-image or was internal, spiritual growth the major player in feeling differently about myself?

My brother Rich had achieved the rank of second lieutenant. After his discharge from the army, he began working with an inner city group in York, the Princess Players. In an effort to reintroduce me to life, he offered me the opportunity to act in a play about race relations. The group was asked to perform a play entitled *The Man Nobody Saw*, by Elizabeth Blake. It was 1970. Lyndon Johnson had recently signed the Civil Rights Act, but that certainly did not instantly mend relations between blacks and whites. This play, contracted by the Pennsylvania South Synod of the Lutheran Church to be performed by the Princess Players, portrayed the plight of a young Afro-American as he attempted to get a job, find decent housing for his family, and simply function in a white dominated society. The purpose of presenting the forty-five-minute play in churches, with primarily white populations, was to bring a dialogue about the issues to the forefront of our white culture.

Besides two or three Afro-Americans, the play required a white man, which role Richard would act, and a white woman. Rich asked me to take that part.

As I became acquainted with the others in the production, I slowly crawled out of my shell of depression. Acting demanded a sense of climbing into someone else's life and skin, temporarily forgetting one's own cares and responsibilities. As I spent many hours with these young people whose lives were so different from my own, and yet primarily similar, my horizons stretched. I began to realize that others face a great deal of uncertainty, too.

The experience was eye opening and taught me that I had a lot to be thankful for.

CHAPTER 29

Breakthrough

Wednesday, August 5, 1970

In high school, as a good, Bible-toting Christian, I was out to witness to the world, to bring everyone to salvation through Jesus Christ. And according to my "Wordless Book," the witnessing begins with the Black Page—all have sinned. We are all sinners, unworthy, undeserving of this great sacrifice of Jesus dying on the cross.

I took this very much to heart. Evangelical preachers helped reinforce this self-loathing, self-reprehension, with their calls to repentance and "we are unworthy" attitudes.

But recently, I have been pondering other words of Jesus—"Love the Lord your God with all your heart and love your neighbor as yourself." We take for granted that our everyday will to live is self-love when so many of us struggle to live from day to day without truly loving ourselves.

I think I know what it means to love my neighbor, but first, I must love myself. I must tell myself, "I am worthy—I am deserving of love, of health, of friendship, of a good and bountiful life."

This continues to be a day to day goal—to love myself. It's easy to find all the undesirable things about me. It is necessary to list what about me is good and deserving. Actually, there need not be a list. I am lovable, deserving, and worthy just by drawing breath.

Peggy

CHAPTER 30

Pushing On

When the performance stint with the Princess Players ended, I obtained work as payroll clerk in one of York's tobacco factories. But by early December, I was ready to get back to school. The eight-to-five workaday routine did not stimulate my creativity. Again, I was questioning where my life was going, what was my purpose in living?

The pastor at our little country church was a social-minded, creative individual, Jesse. He did unorthodox things in the church, like having me sing "I Don't Know How to Love Him" from the new musical *Jesus Christ, Superstar*. One day, as we sat together in the café at the Bon Ton Department Store in downtown York, I expressed my conundrum.

"It's so hard to know what God wants me to do with my life. I just can't see beyond next month, much less plan a career."

Jesse giggled. "Peggy, you just take life too seriously."

His words were like a huge hammer that came barreling against the glass house I had been placed in on that fateful day in March 1964. As this advice became part of my subconscious thinking over the days and years that followed, all the uncertainty turned into possibilities. Fragments of glass fell away at greater and greater velocity. I began to open up to the dream.

Before the end of our conversation that day, Jesse helped me make plans to apply to Lebanon Valley College in a Religious Studies program. I chose this area because Jesse informed me, the United Methodist Church offered a $500 scholarship to students who studied religion, promising to serve in a UMC after graduation. If the student did not serve in the church, the scholarship would automatically become a repayable loan. In those days, tuition at Wheaton had been $3,300 per year. Fees at Lebanon Valley were in a similar range. The money was attractive. Most of my credits from Wheaton transferred. LVC was close enough to home, located in Annville, just outside of Hershey, Pennsylvania. If I wanted, I would be able to go home every weekend. I was excited about going to school, asking questions, talking with fellow classmates about current events, and simply learning about the world I was living in. In spite of taking meds every day, going home for doctors' appointments every three months, and generally paying attention to my health or illness, I was also learning to focus on living.

So in late January 1971, I entered LVC as a second semester sophomore. Although I took a course, Religions in America, that first semester, I never really pursued religious studies after that. My work with the Princess Players had attracted me to acting and the theater. If LVC had a theater major, I would have opted for that. Instead, I majored in English and spent my time studying great writers, putting the religion major to the side. Although I had been extremely homesick when at Wheaton, now that I was closer to home, just knowing that I could go home allowed me to release that anxiety, so that I almost never went home. I participated in stage plays with the drama organization, Wig and Buckle. It was at an audition for one-act plays to be performed during the first annual Spring Arts Festival that I met Steve. He was one of the directors. That first semester, I observed him from a distance. I actually dated several other young men, usually a once or twice thing. My goal was to love life, to enjoy people, but not get too close.

Steve possessed many qualities that attracted me. He was a musician, he had a dulcet tenor voice; he played trumpet, one of my favorite instruments; he played guitar, very musically, not just "strum-a-strum-a-strum," but he delineated phrases and gave life to a song with a variety of strokes and rhythmic emphases. It was the day of Crosby, Stills,

Nash, and Young. He played in a group who performed their songs very well—"Teach Your Children," "Love the One You're With," and "Wooden Ships." He sang Neil Young solos, "Heart of Gold," "Old man take a look at my life, I'm a lot like you..." When I played my Neil Young album at home that summer, Mother asked me, "Is that Steve?"

He was somewhat reserved, not impulsive and brash.

He enjoyed the theater and was a talented actor and director.

He was nice to look at, with his neatly trimmed beard, hazel eyes, fashionably long hair, and tightly developed pole vaulter's body.

When summer came, my brother Rich visited Mount Gretna Playhouse. There, he ran into Steve who was acting on the Gretna stage. Apparently, Steve asked if I was planning to audition for the Wig and Buckle fall play. When Rich came home and told me this, my desire to audition heightened.

Back at college, I started to watch for this handsome new face whenever I would go to the dining room or student lounge or just in my travels around campus. I soon learned where he spent his time and when so that I could just happen to be where he was.

I don't remember just when he began to notice me. That fall, Steve and I were cast as husband and wife in a production of John Osborne's *Look Back in Anger*. As happens in any theater production, we got to know each other very well. By October, Steve asked me out for our first date, a Sinfonia (music fraternity) hayride. There was a sign-up sheet in the music conservatory, which was located in the middle of campus. Conveniently, I could walk through the conservatory on my way to my English lit classes. Every day, I wistfully gazed on the names Steve had written on the hayride sign-up sheet—*Steve and Madge*. I read it again and again. I had been called many names in my life: Margaret, Peggy, Peg, Margie—but never Madge. The most special thing was that Steve had written it.

With each passing day, I fell deeper and deeper in love. Steve was all things wonderful in my eyes.

In December, he invited me to the conservatory formal, a dinner dance held, by the music fraternity, off campus. When I came back to the dorm that evening, I told one of my musician friends Steve had asked me to the event. Marjie squealed, "Wow! That's the next thing to being asked to be engaged!"

Blinded by the excitement of it all, I made a Renaissance-style gold velvet shirt for Steve to match the gold velvet and deep brown crepe gown I made for myself.

In that month, my maternal grandmother, Amy, had a significant stroke. Although she was totally paralyzed, when I visited her in the hospital, I took a swatch of the velvet for her to touch. As I guided her hands across the soft material, I told her about the young man I had met and how kind and gentle he was.

In January 1972, Grandma Amy died. I went home for the funeral. That morning, I had a terrible headache so I took an Alka-Seltzer. The day was a blur, very sad. The next morning, I felt extremely nauseated. When I vomited into the toilet, there was bright red blood. Not just streaks of blood, but a rush of blood. When I stopped vomiting and called for Mother, I could feel the blood dripping into my stomach. I knew it wouldn't be long before my stomach would fill and I would need to throw up again.

Mother, attempting to remain calm, phoned the doctor who told her to take me to the emergency room immediately. We grabbed a bucket for the trip to the hospital, and I slowly faded into the air. I remember hearing the doctor say to an ER nurse, "Get me the biggest needle you have, STAT! We've got to get this blood into her fast. Double check Type A positive."

I was placed in ICU, where I drifted in and out of consciousness. An endoscopy was performed to determine the source of the bleeding.

I learned that internal bleeding typically occurs in one with advanced liver disease. Since the liver is so scarred (cirrhosed) from the disease, blood can no longer flow through it as usual. So the blood pressure builds and blood is shunted through alternative paths. Commonly, in the liver patient, the blood is forced through veins in the esophagus. Since those veins are not fashioned to accommodate this increased amount of flow and pressure, they become swollen (esophageal varices) and break open. The released blood flows into the stomach, which causes nausea and vomiting, or if it is a slow bleed, the blood goes through the digestive system and is excreted in the stool. The stool is black and tarry. Both bleeds lead to fatigue, dizziness, weakness, and disorientation.

The only solution is blood transfusion. I am fortunate that my blood type is common, A-positive. I am also fortunate that many caring people gave their blood for me. A further blessing is that the blood I received was not contaminated. This first hemorrhage and transfusion occurred in 1971, some years before blood was closely screened for AIDS.

After a brief hospital sojourn, I returned to college and resumed studies. By then, I was a second semester junior. I was taking 10 milligrams of prednisone per day and weighed 128 pounds. Steve was in his senior year. One evening, a speaker came to campus and gave a presentation on the power of alpha waves. Apparently, there are several levels of consciousness defined as: 1) beta waves: our usual, functioning, waking state of being; 2) theta waves: a more relaxed state, not quite as deep as 3) delta waves, a sleeping state of being; 4) alpha waves experienced in the meditative state of being. With alpha waves, we are connected to our surroundings and the present moment and, trite as it may sound, the Universe. The speaker suggested that we all use our minds far from its greatest potential. Practice using alpha waves and we can grasp the powers of the Universe, the energy we so often ignore, and use it to affect ourselves and each other.

This was my first introduction to the idea that our thoughts are powerful enough to influence our health, our relationships, even the very direction of our lives. I read Herman Hesse's *Siddharta* and *The Glass Bead Game* and Richard Bach's *Jonathan Livingston Seagull*. Each of these works had a profound impact on my views of religion and the way I saw my place in this world.

Steve and I spent a great deal of time together, backstage, and whenever we had the opportunity throughout the day and into the night. One evening, walking back to the dorm from rehearsal on a cool, clear night, we both saw a falling star streak through the still sky. This, to me, was some sort of sign. We were falling in love with each other. I was compelled to tell him, "Steve, I'm not sure this is a good thing. Well, I mean, it is a good thing, but I'm not sure it's the best thing for you. I don't know how much longer I'll be around. My health could fail me almost any time. I don't want you to jeopardize your life by having me in it."

He replied, "I'll take the chance. I want to be with you, even if it's just for today."

So the relationship continued to grow.

In February 1972, during semester break, the LVC Jazz band, in which Steve played trumpet, went on tour. I was admitted to Thomas Jefferson University Hospital in Philadelphia for a liver biopsy. The jazz band had a gig at a Philadelphia hotel. The evening of their performance, I phoned the hotel from my hospital bed. I told the concierge the situation: that I was hospitalized but was very interested in a certain trumpet player and would really like to hear the band. The concierge obliged me by holding the phone so that I could listen to the sounds of trumpets and saxophones playing "Birdland" by the great Quincy Jones. This was a little oasis in my experience of liver biopsy. My dear, faithful mother traveled the 106 miles (one way) in harsh winter blizzard to be with me for a few hours, then traveled all the way back home by herself.

She often related the story of the fierce winter storm piling snow on the roads and blinding her as she drove in the dark. Somewhere on that trip, she found herself behind a snow plow, clearing the path before her.

"I just stayed behind him so I knew where I was going. When we got to the Glen Rock exit off I83, I put on my right turn signal." She wipes away a tear. "That dear man got off the highway and cleared my way the whole way home."

How cared for I have been.

The doctors learned very little from that biopsy. The experience was, again, not very pleasant. I remember, just down the hall from me was a young man who had major burns all over his body. As nurses moved him to take him to the whirlpool, I heard him scream and moan. I never saw him, but Mother told me that get-well cards had been plastered all over the mirror in his room so he could not see himself.

When I returned to college a week later, everything seemed normal to me. I became involved in another show, *Man of La Mancha*, in which Steve played the priest and I ran properties. I made a special suede-covered prayer book for him. We spent a lot of offstage time cuddling in the theater darkness.

Steve graduated that spring.

On June 17, 1972, my sister Kathy married her sweetheart Russ on the lawn at our Glen Rock home. I was not only one of her brides-maids, but Steve and I and our pianist friend, Bob Moul, sang and played music for the wedding.

A few days after the wedding, June 21, Steve and I went with brother Rich and his girlfriend, Jamie, to a movie theater in York to see *A Clockwork Orange*. When we came out of the theater, the rain was pouring in torrents. Streets were swamped with water. We did not know it then, but this was the beginning of the historic flood from Hurricane Agnes. Sometime, in the blur of all of this chaos, I received a phone call from my gastroenterologist, Dr. William B. Thorsen. He told me my latest blood work indicated that I was pregnant. Close to three months. He demanded that I schedule with my gynecologist admission to the hospital for a D&C as soon as possible.

You may wonder how this was possible since I've reported that my period stopped when I was twelve years old. After taking prednisone and stabilizing the liver disease, my body started menstruating again. As I recall, I was a sophomore in high school, age fifteen.

Steve and I told no one but Rich and Jesse about the pregnancy. I did not want my parents to stress over yet another health issue for me. Besides that, I was terrified of the lectures they would have for me. I was already regretting our carelessness and the loss of my child's impending life. Those couple of days I was in York Hospital, Steve slept in the car in the parking lot. He was by my side whenever allowable. We talked about trusting each other and convinced each other that this was the best move. Dr. Thorsen declared that, without abortion, I would die before the pregnancy came to term and that the baby would be abnor-mal. When I awoke from the anesthesia after the procedure, I felt a definite loss of life. It was heartbreaking.

Steve stayed with me through all of this. He, too, experienced the pain of loss.

In the fall, he played a role in a Harrisburg Playhouse produc-tion of *1776*. Someone in the cast suggested he apply for a position as assistant band director in the West Shore school district. I stood beside him as he shaved his beard at the bathroom sink in his parents' East

Petersburg home. It was the first time I had seen him without a beard. He looked so much younger and so sweet. Oh, and he got the job.

To my amazement, I graduated college on a sunny day in May 1973. I had lived through it all and was twenty-two years old. Doctors had told me I may not see twenty-one. I was learning to give thanks for each new day. The next challenge was to enter the workforce and earn my own living. *Earn my own living.* Interesting phrase. Hadn't I already done that? By serving as test subject guinea pig for curious doctors, as patient for ICU nurses, and by completing a demanding course of college studies?

As President Sample of Lebanon Valley College presented me with my degree, the bachelor of arts in English, he smiled. "See you at work tomorrow?"

In that final semester as a senior, I had requested and received an independent study course in journalism. No journalism studies were then offered in LVC's regular English curriculum. My love and strength was writing. So my coach, Dr. John Kearney, gave me assignments that placed me in close contact with LVC's public relations office. Director Ann Montieth appreciated my work and enthusiasm. She offered me a job as associate in PR upon my graduation.

So indeed, I would be reporting to work as an employee for the college in the public relations office that Monday following Sunday's graduation. I had a room in one of the dorm houses that remained open for the summer. Actually, I spent very little time there. It was mostly a place for me to stash my stuff. As soon as I got off work, I walked three or four blocks to the apartment Steve shared with his friend and former college roomie, Joe. It was there I spent most nights.

Work at the PR office was stimulating enough. I wrote a Parents' Newsletter, items on students' accomplishments, an item about my friend Don Frantz, who was playing a white gorilla at Hershey Park. That summer, another friend, Tom, initiated "Lebanon Valley Summer Theater." I played roles in *A Funny Thing Happened on the Way to the Forum* and in *The Rainmaker*. Steve played major roles in both. So I was able to create feature pieces for local newspapers in York and Lancaster counties to publicize the shows. However, by late August, I had had enough of Lebanon Valley and Annville. Although I don't know exactly what I was looking for, I resigned my position at the college and went home to live in the country again. A local temporary work agency found various positions for me. Rich found a lovely little brick house that he and Steve rented in East York. I moved in with them.

Then I applied to be an administrative secretary for the vice president of a wholesale foods company, P.A. & S. Small. My boss was happy that I could simply take notes about what he wanted to convey in a letter and then create a well-worded piece of communication. I did a lot of typing and filing there.

Steve and Rich continued to be involved in theater together, with the York Recreation Commission and Hanover Playhouse. As summer approached, Tom invited Steve to play several roles in the Lebanon Valley Summer Theater. I also auditioned for *Company*. Tom cast me in the role of Amy who sings, "Getting Married Today." Steve and I had decided in May to be married before summer's end. So after about a week of rehearsal and tons of stress trying to learn lines and plan a wedding, I left the play.

I ordered a pattern for my unique wedding dress from a magazine. Before it was pieced together, my mother and I embroidered the skirt of muslin in a pattern of wheat heads, Queen Anne's lace, mushrooms, and cattails. Attempting to create a Renaissance look, I designed and sewed dresses for the bride's maids and flower girl. Each dress had a yellow bodice with an earth-hued flowered long skirt. I sewed white shirts with cross-stringed closings and brown faux-suede vests for the groom and groomsmen. One of my neighbors made the cake, which was a work of architecture tiered in carrot and date layers, with Frangelico, triple sec, and other fruity liqueurs sprinkled on the separating icing. The entire structure was lathered in sweet coffee-flavored frosting, edged with chocolate. Finally, the cake was decorated with tiny mushroom meringues and wheat heads to tie into the wedding dress theme.

On a sweltering August day, a little more than a year after I graduated from college, Steve and I were married in an outdoor ceremony at my Glen Rock home. It was a dream come true.

College Graduate 1973

Father and Bride, August 24, 1974

"If I could surround you with all my love,
I'd sing to the sun; I'd pray to the moon,
Knowing that God is at home in you."

The Happy Couple

CHAPTER 31

New Hope

I learned to enjoy life. Who knew how long I would be around?

I worked another two years with P.A. & S. Small. In addition to my regular duties, I researched the company's history, how two brothers, native to York County, carried on their father's enterprising spirit and supplied food to grocery stores in the county and beyond. The family had been in York since before the revolutionary war. I found a little read diary in the Martin Memorial Library that provided great insight into the tenacity of spirit in the family. The only remaining brother, Philip, at that time, owned a game ranch in Africa. One of my assignments was to list the inventory of animals living there.

The company held a contest for its retail food chain customers to purchase product enough to travel on a business trip to Acapulco. One day, my boss, the company vice president, called me into his office.

"You and Steve went where for your honeymoon in August?"

I smiled, wondering why he was asking this question. "We had a great time travelling down Skyline Drive in Virginia. The pup tent was a bit cramped, but the scenery was breathtaking."

"How would you and Steve like to travel with us to Acapulco for a real honeymoon?" he offered.

That evening, I suggested to Steve that we eat at one of our favorite restaurants after he finished teaching. Over stuffed flounder and Chablis, I told him about the Acapulco trip scheduled for mid-April. A chartered flight, breakfast and dinner provided, housing in the Hyatt-Regency Hotel, all at no cost to us except lunches and extras we may purchase. What a gift this was to newly graduated college students, paying off college debt and struggling to meet the bills.

Steve's brow furrowed. "I don't know. That's just the time school spring concerts begin."

My heart stopped. "What are you saying? This is a once in a lifetime opportunity! When will we ever be offered a trip like this again? Surely, your concerts can wait a week!"

We skipped dessert as he agreed to ask about taking a week off in April. Later that spring, as Steve conducted his suburban elementary students singing, "Reuben, Reuben, I've Been Thinking," he sported a brightly colored tie he obtained from a wares hawker on the Santa Lucia beach.

In 1975, York initiated its now annual Olde York Street Fair, which occurs on Mother's Day. I created press releases concerning art and artisans, also highlighting musical and drama acts as well as food vendors and street performers. Little did I know it, but this on the job training was preparing me for later work in public relations.

Steve and I moved into a semidetached home on Chestnut Street in York with Rich and his new wife, Jamie. As cultural arts director for the city, she was required to live within city limits. Steve and I needed a place to live, and as a new homeowner, Rich was happy for us to split the expenses.

The four of us became involved with various community entertainments. Rich, Steve, and I acted in a show at York Little Theater about William Shakespeare called *A Cry of Players*, by William Gibson, directed by Bert Smith. I played Will's mistress and had a scene where we rolled around onstage, kissing and hugging. It was the first experience I had kissing someone who smoked cigarettes. Not pleasant. I understood the saying that kissing a smoker is like putting your mouth into an ashtray! Jamie and I volunteered to participate in a variety show for the Young Women's Club of York. Although I do not recall who directed the show, I remember being assigned the Japanese folksong, "Sakura." More a Judy Collins fan, it was not my cup of tea, so to speak, but we had a great deal of fun performing. Additionally, that year, Jamie and I were cast in a locally written play, *The Distaff Side*, a creative depiction of the wives of members of the Continental Congress who, on November 17, 1777, adopted the Articles of Confederation in York, Pennsylvania. We performed the play in the Historic Old York County Courthouse, seated at the tables where those history-making men had sat and fashioned the rules on which to base our country's rights and privileges. I played Mrs. John Witherspoon of New Jersey.

Rich began teaching acting classes in a little unused building in downtown York. There, I learned many valuable lessons that were applicable to my daily living: onstage, it is necessary to be aware of the space and objects around the actor so that she can move freely without colliding with other actors or set pieces; in daily life, awareness of space is valuable in keeping me safe from bashing into a coffee table or tree stump. I learned, too, that each of us is consumed with our own issues, whether our appearance or abilities. We are so self-conscious, wondering what other people are thinking about us, when, actually, those other people are occupied with their own self-consciousness, not really paying that much attention to us. When I became aware of this, there was a release of energy which I could then direct toward joy and thanksgiving in living.

Rich also sought for us outside opportunities to learn. One of these was a session called *Energy Body Workshop*. During this workshop at University of Maryland, eminent aikido practitioner, George Leonard, instructed class attendees to break up into pairs. As one of the pair lay on the floor, Mr. Leonard guided them into a state of deep relaxation. Then, that one of the pair was told to bend their elbow, elevating their hand. Meanwhile, the other of the pair sat on the floor beside their relaxed partner. The seated one was instructed to gently grasp their partner's hand and to press on the back of the hand, bending the wrist to its extreme. As the relaxed person experienced discomfort, Mr. Leonard instructed, "Breathe through the pain, saying, 'Thank you. More,'" asking for more pressure. Little did I know it then, but this exercise of relaxing into the pain would play a huge role in future experiences.

Steve and I moved to a cottage on a 150-acre farm in southern York County. We lived on Sycamore Lane, so called because the farm boasted the county's largest sycamore tree. We enjoyed makeshift dinners around the Franklin stove, baking potatoes in aluminum foil, warming a pot of beans on top. Our musician friends came to spend the evening playing guitars and banjo. There was a real white picket fence around the house. Horses grazed in the meadow by the pond. It was a storybook home.

One morning, I awoke feeling ill and nauseated. I say *ill* meaning that, in addition to the nausea, I had a sense of something just not right. Very early in the morning, I went to the bathroom to vomit in the toilet. The extrusion was dark red blood. Too tired to call Steve from bed, I grabbed the white ceramic basin and lay on the rag rug outside the bathroom door. I continued to make trips to the toilet to vomit, then lay on the rug. When Steve found me there around 6:30 in the morning, he phoned the doctor. He must have contacted my mother as well because, as I recall, she came to our house. As Steve drove me to the hospital, she followed in her car.

As usual during these episodes, I do not remember many details. I do remember that, after I was discharged from the hospital having received at least six units of blood, I had an unusual experience. (As if bleeding into one's gut isn't unusual enough!)

Throughout my life, I struggled with the problem of faith and healing. By this time, I was twenty-seven years old. I had lived with chronic liver disease for nearly fifteen years. People suggested that I go to a faith-healing service performed by Kathryn Kuhlman. People prayed for my healing for years and years.

I have always wondered if I had enough faith to be healed.

What if you believe, but when visiting the doctor, he says you are still sick? Does that mean your faith wasn't strong enough or that you doubted and, therefore, were not worthy of healing?

One morning, shortly after I came home from the hospital after this particular bleeding incident, I awoke feeling full of hope. I lay in bed and began to pray. I gave thanks for the healing I was experiencing. I wondered if the woman who touched the hem of Jesus's garment and felt the surge of his healing power course through her felt like I was feeling now. I was overcome with a sense of warmth and wellness.

In light of the fact that twenty years later I was pronounced in end stage liver disease, I suppose that moment was not the healing miracle I had hoped. However, the experience filled me with light and a renewed love of life. So in the end, it was a healing experience, another opportunity to give thanks.

CHAPTER 32

A New Name

To my chagrin, Rich and Jamie divorced in December 1975. Jamie and I always had fun together, but you never know the dynamics of a relationship unless you are in it, so I certainly could not discern the reason for their split. We left our country home on Sycamore Lane to move in with Rich and help with mortgage and utilities. In the following months, Rich allowed himself the opportunity to explore theater opportunities. He, along with Steve, Tim, and I, formed Gallimaufry Productions. Besides teaching classes, Rich negotiated with the Yorktowne Hotel to realize their first and only dinner theater. The four of us gathered props, created press releases, rehearsed, built sets, and made or collected costumes for *Jacque Brel Is Alive and Well and Living in Paris,* *Luv* by Murray Schisgal, and *I Do, I Do* the musical by Jones and Schmidt. We were so busy, we didn't have time to be exhausted!

When our theater activity at the Yorktowne ended sometime in 1977, I was again unemployed. The ever-faithful temp agency placed me at Crispus Attucks to work briefly as secretary to the Director of Day Care Services. When the director discovered my efficiency and professionalism, she negotiated with the employment agency to hire me full-time. The work was interesting as I had the opportunity to meet children and their parents. I enjoyed writing letters and summaries of activity for the director.

In 1979, Gallimaufry Productions, Inc. began producing and performing plays in York and Lancaster Counties. Ephrata's Legion Star Playhouse was failing financially and in attracting audiences. A small group of interested Ephrata residents invested their own funds to bring in different performers every week in the summer. They tried desperately to keep the theater afloat. It was a golden opportunity for Rich to negotiate a deal which made Gallimaufry the resident performing group. In consultation with invested community members, we renamed the theater, The Playhouse in the Park. A local artist created a lovely logo, which included a spreading hardwood tree. This is where Rich met Su, his true love, who had been managing the playhouse the year before we arrived.

For the next six years, we were insanely busy as Rich directed all of us in a plethora of plays, including *The Apple Tree*, *On Borrowed Time*, *The Lion in Winter*, and *The Secret Affairs of Mildred Wild*. Rich suggested that rather than my nickname, Peggy, I use the stage name *Garet*. As a theater student at Penn State, he had a professor who was Margaret, but went by Garet. At almost age thirty, I was ready for some new energy, and so it was. Garet became the name by which the Lancaster Newspaper reviewers knew me. Since it had become my stage name, it naturally followed that, when I wrote a one-woman show of my own in the mid-nineties, I used the name Garet as a penname. Since that time, my Lancaster County friends, for the most part knew me as Garet. Those on the west side of the Susquehanna continue to refer to me as Peggy, my childhood through early adulthood name.

But I digress…

DREAM

*T*he place seems friendly enough. There are people laughing. People who feel like friends. My upper arms feel warm, like they are being held gently. Steve, my husband and best friend, is on the other side of the room. He is engaged in conversation with a group of people, probably other actors who share his interests.

I gradually notice someone strange enter the room. He does not belong. He is cajoling, threatening. He moves among the guests, laughing, charming each one he stops to talk with. But a tightness is gripping my chest.

A voice within me is screaming, "Look out! Danger!" I try to catch Steve's eye to tell him we must leave, now. But he does not see me. I move toward him. The group surrounds him, blocking my path. I am on the fringes of his collection of friends. Finally, he glances my way.

"We have to go now," I try to be polite. He continues his conversation. I move into the group and grab his arm. "Come on, Steve, we really must leave right now."

It is as if he does not hear me. I signal to the group, without words, that this newcomer is big trouble. The tension in my chest is mounting. We need, all of us, to get out of here, now!

But I am mute. No one has heard me. I am invisible. What I have said makes no impact. Are these people blind? Can they not see that danger approaches?

In frustration, I fall to the floor. I cannot move. I cannot respond.

Perhaps someone will pay attention now. Perhaps now I will be taken seriously. Perhaps now I will be of some value.

And I awaken.

CHAPTER 33

Poor Sick Girl

In 1978, as I struggled to work full-time at Crispus Attucks, my sister-in-law Suanne urged me to apply to the Social Security Administration for disability support. I had begun to suffer from severe edema (fluid retention) in my legs. After an eight-hour day at the office, I habitually came home, lay on the couch, and elevated my legs until bedtime. As the week progressed, it was more and more difficult to recover. Even though Dr. Thorsen prescribed diuretics, my elimination could not counterbalance the swelling.

As seems to happen routinely when one applies for disability, I applied and was denied. Our federal congressman, whom I had known since childhood, was a member of the small church where I had attended. With Suanne's help, I asked him for his advocacy in appealing this denial. In February 1981, I was adjudicated legally disabled.

I left Crispus Attucks in 1980, largely due to the toll working full-time was taking on my health. Erratic income then came from a variety of part-time employment through temp agencies.

Although I now had more time to be with Steve and a more flexible schedule to write and play piano and sing and act, I was disappointed that I could not earn a substantial salary. Once again, my body had put me in a subnormal position.

CHAPTER 34

Metamorphosis of Vision

N ow, I must confess that by the time I enrolled in studies at Lebanon Valley College, I rarely attended church.

While at Wheaton College, as mentioned previously, I was exposed to multiple denominations of the Christian faith. Pentecostal, Episcopal, Baptist, United Church of Christ, Plymouth Brethren, Catholic, and United Methodist congregations all professed to worship the same God. However, even within a given body of worshippers, there were differences of interpretation of the Bible and the personage(s) of God. I began to consider that God, the Source of all, is truly indefinable, unimaginable, that all these -isms put that Infinite Power into little boxes.

Hadn't I already been gifted with life again and again? Through no effort, no merit of my own? And hadn't I been misled by well-meaning evangelists and committed Christians into a psychology of despising myself and personifying God with human attributes?

As I opened my heart and my mind to various ways of interpreting God or whatever name you wish to place upon that most omnipotent, omnipresent, all-seeing Force, my heart and mind also welcomed more people into my experience. People who had different backgrounds from mine, who may have been generally considered unusual. People with kind and giving spirits who lived differently, worshipped differently, thought differently than I.

I found community in the theater. A stage play is the perfect situation for a group of people to become "one body." Each person is dependent upon the other to execute the correct blocking and script. And if that doesn't happen because someone forgets their line or drops a vase or misses their entrance cue, then we depend upon our own and our fellow's ability to improvise. Isn't that what life is as well? A series of improvisations. My reaction to your statement or your action and your reaction to mine. And in working on the stage, you learn that you have choices in those reactions. I can deliver anger or warmth or apathy. I have a choice in the outcome of that given situation.

The plays themselves, the creations of the playwrights, spoke to everyday life experiences. Audiences experienced frustration, difficult hurdles, gratifying joy. And as the curtain fell, there were lessons learned, thoughts provoked, conversations begun.

For me, this was true worship. Gradually, I learned to love myself more, and in doing so, I was able to love others more, to empathize with their experience, to help in some way when I could.

I have never totally dissociated from basic Christian principles. The Bible states in Proverbs 22:6 (NIV), "*Start children off on the way they should go, and even when they are old they will not turn from it.*" Modern psychologists say that a child's formative years are from birth to age four. From age five years and onward, that initial formation may be influenced by further instruction and experiences, but an imprint has been made and retained. I was raised in a loving, nurturing home where prayer and church and Christ were central, and so I find it natural to integrate much of what I learned in those early years into my life. However, as Jesus practiced tolerance and taught us that the Kingdom of God is within us (Luke 17:21, NIV), I am pressed to entertain many ways of expressing God. My spiritual life is expansive, ever willing to explore new proposals. After all, isn't the Source in everything?

Could I be sensing echoes of my Native American heritage joined with my Swiss German Protestant ancestry? Could it be that, in this life, I have learned that each of us can suffer the same pain, emotionally and physically, that we aren't really very different from one another?

Certainly, my life has been saved by those of various faith professions—Protestant, Sikh, Buddhist, Hindi, and Catholic. My God permeates the entire world and all people therein. Only when we place God into little boxes, when we limit that Source with personification and definition, does conflict arise. The measure of validity rests only in Love. Is this thought or action for the good of all concerned?

Through all the illness and challenges in my life, I have found that strength lies within. It is good to nurture our Center through meditation, whatever that means for you. We have the opportunity to find within ourselves great treasure.

The Dream is what we make of it.

CHAPTER 35

Parents, Sort Of

I n those years when we were involved in Ephrata doing theater, Steve and I found another little country home to rent on Croll School Road surrounded by York County farmland. It seemed we were always short on money. In addition to directing both vocal and bell choir at York's Otterbein United Methodist Church, Steve taught a few private music students in our tiny cottage. Many was the time, as I busied myself reading or folding laundry in the next room, I heard the squeaking strains of "The Volga Boatmen" on novice clarinet or violin.

In spite of my physical limitations, I felt the need to contribute financially as well. I found a position as part-time church secretary at nearby Otterbein United Methodist Church of Spry. The job itself was relatively untaxing—answer phone, create Sunday morning bulletins, format and produce a monthly newsletter, prepare mailings, and other clerical duties. The congregation also availed themselves of our musical skills. Steve and I provided entertainment as we sang together to his own guitar accompaniment for a Valentine's banquet. I sang a solo for a church service. In the summers, Steve and I acted and helped with various phases of theater production at Ephrata's Playhouse in the Park with Gallimaufry Productions. All this activity, coupled with singing with the choir Steve was directing in York, took its toll on my fragile health.

I noticed that my stools became black and tarry looking, and I was feeling lightheaded and dizzy. I confessed to Steve I may need to call the doctor.

I was admitted to York Hospital. In another dreamlike state, nurses and doctors came and went. Occasionally, I saw a familiar face—Steve, my mother, my father, Jesse, Kathy, Tim, or Richard. Their voices were comforting to me, but it was difficult to retain a coherent thought much less carry on a meaningful conversation.

Again, I received six units of blood. Later, when I was able to attend choir practice and shared this information with a soprano who was a nurse, she said, "Six units! That's approximately the amount of blood anyone normally has circulating in their veins!"

After four days in the hospital, I was discharged. I rested at home for a week or two, then returned to my part-time job at the church. I added to my already taxing schedule by playing organ for worship at Bethlehem UMC in downtown York. A Sunday morning in those days consisted of the service at Bethlehem at 9 a.m., leaving immediately following the postlude and travelling the ten blocks to Otterbein UMC for Steve to direct the choir and me to sing alto in the group.

On the evening of November 27, 1979, I was at the organ in Bethlehem church practicing for Advent. Since I was alone in the big church, in the midst of downtown York, I made a habit of locking the door after I entered. I was playing "O Come, O Come, Emmanuel" when there came a loud knocking on the heavy wooden door. As I walked down the center aisle to the side door, the main entrance to the church, I wondered, who may need to come here when there were no activities scheduled? Could this be someone in need looking for assistance at the house of God? Could it be a burglar, ready to attack whoever opened the door and then ransack the building?

The knocking was persistent. Suddenly, it seemed, I was God's representative. As I turned the brass knob to open the door, I prayed for strength and a loving heart. To my surprise, instead of a family poorly dressed with sniffling children in hand or a couple of teenage boys ready to shove me to the side to rob the church, there stood my brother-in-law, Russ, a look of tension on his face.

"Kathy's water broke. The baby's on its way. You wanna come to our house now?"

It was more a statement than a question.

Kathy and Russ had already had our first niece, Amy, just two years before. A few hours after she was born at York Hospital, as he was driving home for some much needed sleep, Russ stopped by Crispus Attucks Community Center to inform me of the good news. It was November 22, 1977. I was still working there on South Duke Street as full-time administrative secretary to the director of day care services. That day, Russ sat in my office to tell me he was the new father of a healthy baby girl named Amy Beth—Amy for Grandma Amy Masimore, Mother's mother, and Beth after Daddy's mother, Anna Elizabeth. Did he see my joy at this happy announcement shadowed by my disappointment that I could not give my mother and father their first grandchild? Or that, had my baby lived, I fantasized naming her Amy? (Although I was never told the sex of my child the day of that dreadful D and C, I was certain the tiny life inside me was a girl.) Or that my baby's birthday would have been around this time, the end of November?

When they became pregnant with their second child, two years later, Kathy and Russ decided to have a home birth. They attended classes and found a midwife in a nearby Maryland community who agreed to deliver the child.

When Kathy had reached her sixth month of carrying this child, Russ asked Steve and me if we would be present at the birth. Steve's duty was to care for two-year-old Amy. I was to assist in any way necessary. Although he never said so, I believe Russ was giving us this opportunity since he knew we would never be able to have our own child.

So on this night in November, Russ stood before me telling me the time was at hand. He returned to the car where Kathy was waiting. As they started for home, I quickly stashed my music in my case and drove (actually flew) to get Steve, wherever he was (I do not remember). We arrived at the Walker's home just before the midwife, who after entering immediately ordered us to boil some water. How clichéd was that?

The remainder of the night was far from clichéd as all that occurred was completely outside of our experience. Such a gift it was to witness the miracle of birth.

Five years later, October 21, 1984, to be exact, Steve and I were privileged to witness the home birth of my brother Tim's second child. It was a truly unforgettable, electrically charged experience, a gift we continue to treasure.

At one point in the early '80s, shortly after we moved into our little house in Columbia, Steve and I seriously considered adoption. He was working steadily as an actor and musician; I had obtained a full-time job at Elizabethtown College as faculty secretary. Things seemed relatively stable, financially. We enrolled in an adoption course and attended several sessions. Between the uncertainties and waiting involved in adoption and the fact that I again suffered a bleeding episode, we decided adoption was not a good idea for us or for a child. I knew I did not want to have a child in our care and suddenly leave this life and Steve, alone, to raise the little one.

So although we never bore a child, we had been twice part of that indescribable phenomenon. My brothers and sister further gave us the gift of spending time with their children as they grew. We were the fun aunt and uncle who read books to them on demand, played board games and ball and hide 'n' seek. We ate together while watching TV, *The Animaniacs* or *Care Bears*, chomping pizza, mac and cheese, and popsicles.

I never knew the joy of children conceived by my husband and me, but my dream of being a parent had, in a lovely sense, been fulfilled.

Sisters 1994

CHAPTER 36

Surviving

We participated fully at Otterbein United Methodist Church in York, Steve as choir director, me singing alto with the choir. We were attending church while not fully buying into all that was professed there. I had been increasingly exposed to Eastern ways of thinking—Taoism, transcendentalism. All-inclusive ways of thinking—me as part of a huge plan, a massive cosmos. It was not difficult for me to merge this with the omnipotence of Christianity's God. I did not *not* believe in much of Christian thought. I simply did not purport myself to be Christian.

Nevertheless, just prior to Lent, the council of ministries chairperson, also a soprano with the choir, solicited brief writings for a devotional book for the congregation. I decided to share some of my own experience. The reading was for March 18, 1984, a little more than twenty years following my first hospitalization:

Your Faith Can Make You Whole
Mark 5:25–34

Twenty years later and I should be but a memory…a thirteen-year-old girl whom family and friends wept over and pushed into their "used-to-be's" when she fell asleep for the last time.

Twenty years have passed since the doctors told my mother and father on a cold gray day in March, they would not be taking their little girl home with them again—ever.

But people prayed as the family watched the jaundiced child hold tight to life.

Twenty years later and I am a walking miracle. I am the child of a Creator capable of wonders I cannot comprehend as a little human being—wonders happening around and in us every day. Although no one has handed me a "clean bill of health," every day, I visualize myself as completely healed. I believe that I am whole.

A glorious thrill overcomes me when I simply thank God that I am His child—what more does one need to be whole?

I continued to develop a healthier attitude about my life. I may not have followed the path I envisioned when I was attending Wheaton, but to the astonishment of doctors, I was still living!

I remained active in the theater, helping with props, costumes, and other technical work. I worked in promoting shows for CoMotion, a small alternative theater company, and acted with the Actors' Company of Pennsylvania and Theater of the Seventh Sister. With Steve's help, I also adapted for the stage poetry written by one of my former English profs and produced it in play-like fashion at CoMotion. I wrote and performed a one-woman play about the conflict in El Salvador entitled *Chepe: One Day of Life*, which I performed in more than thirty venues, from churches to civic organizations and colleges to the actual theater in Theater of the Seventh Sister's local artist series.

My love of writing coupled with my performance skills led me into the area of storytelling. I entertained with my own stories and a few adapted tales for the annual Jane Mohr Memorial Award banquet, New Life for Children, Family Day at Long Park, and CoMotion Theatre.

The passionate, straight and narrow, evangelical girl of the mid-sixties had transformed into an open, welcoming artist. The theater was my church, the venue where inspiration came upon me through story, conflicting idea, and community.

Storyteller
CoMotion Theater 1997

Portrayal of Rose Hoffman
In *Working*, Theater of
the Seventh Sister
1996

School for Husbands
TSS
1998

DREAM

I am under obligation to participate in an autopsy of sorts.

The medical examiner is a young woman with shoulder-length blonde hair. From the corner of my eye, in my peripheral vision, I know she is carefully cutting and removing the top layers of skin with a scissors.

When she asks me to count the lines in the hand, I tell her, "I don't know if I can do this." But I know I must try.

So she places the hand of the corpse in mine. To my surprise, the small delicate hand is not cold and cemented, but so warm I almost feel it move/ respond to my careful touch. The hand is approximately the size of my own, with a small triangle of flesh removed.

I look to her face, a pleasant, peaceful smile planted there. Who was this young woman and why was she no longer vibrantly alive?

I quickly count the lines and turn away, my stomach convulsing in nausea.

Then, I am asked to conclude by counting the horizontal lines in the face, where again, flesh has been removed. This is more difficult as they seem to have been darkened by ashes or some kind of marking. I look to the ME, and she has the same kind of dark markings.

"How many?"

I am really not certain of anything except that I cannot look at the marred flesh again.

"Twenty," I reply hastily. And feel sorrowful that this person could not have been my friend in life.

She, in death, seemed to have more compassion than the ME who was just going about her business.

I was sad to leave the beautiful maiden of death, even to be free of my obligation and escape from there to life.

And yet, I awaken…

CHAPTER 37

Evaluation

On that day in Dr. Srour's office as he gave me a choice of transplant facilities, University of Pennsylvania in Philadelphia, Pittsburgh, or Johns Hopkins in Baltimore, I chose Baltimore. Interstate Route 83 runs from Harrisburg through York and Southern York County, through Northern Maryland and right into Baltimore. Interstate 83 is directly accessible via a twenty-minute drive over Pennsylvania Route 30 from Lancaster County, where we live. Most of my husband's family lived in Lancaster County. My mother and father and siblings and their families lived in Southern York County and Harrisburg. So my quick, uninformed decision that day was based entirely upon geography, the most easily accessible routes for my future visitors.

Now, the first significant event was in progress—evaluation for transplant candidacy. Steve and I were traveling the sixty-four miles, over the Susquehanna River, through eastern York County, to 183, and south to Baltimore. Although as Steve drove, we barely spoke, the chatter in my brain was nearly nonstop.

Johns Hopkins University Medical Center. The very name shouted to me: prestigious, cutting edge (as in research, not necessarily surgery, although that, too), brilliant physicians, and state-of-the-art technology. What would this Dr. Anna Mae Diehl need to do to me? What would we see on the way to her office? Would we encounter patients sicker than I am? How soon could I expect the surgery?

The surgery! Crunchy shards of ice rattled through my veins at the thought. To remove my liver and replace it with someone else's required major cutting! Did I really want this? Also, wouldn't someone I don't even know have to die before I could get the liver? How could I live with that death on my conscience? Maybe this was just a bad idea.

I know my illness has always been a burden of deep concern for my parents. I think Mother truly wants this, but what about Daddy? Yes, he would prefer I live rather than die. But in his heart of hearts, he has always been one to "let nature take its course." He has taught me that God has a plan in my illness.

Already, throughout high school, I had clung to the promises in the Holy Bible:

"Come to me…I will give you rest."

"My burden is light."

"Nothing can separate us from the Love of God."

"Your faith (can) make you whole."

I was open to sharing my faith with others by singing at church and in Youth for Christ. Not only had I sung before the twenty-five to fifty young people and adults in the social room of the New Freedom fire hall and in local churches, but I sang before hundreds at the Eastern Regional gathering of Youth for Christ in Ocean City, New Jersey. Those who heard me always expressed inspiration. After all, they conjectured, at age sixteen or seventeen, I had "already been through so much."

So after all this, why should we interfere in God's (nature's) plan? One would think, since I had been sick for thirty-four years, I would have had several surgeries. Fortunately, however, the scalpel was relatively absent in my life.

At age twenty-eight, I was hospitalized to have my wisdom teeth removed. Piece of cake. Friends had prepared me by warning, "You won't have as much pain if you just drink lots of soda afterward. And gum. Keep chewing and chewing gum." Well, I didn't do either of those things, per se. Instead, I drank lots of water and kept moving my jaw. The doctors were amazed that I had little bleeding and no pain.

Some years later, on a routine mammogram, a pea-sized lump was detected in my left breast. A lumpectomy was performed. This minor surgery required an overnight stay in the hospital, probably for safety purposes due to my complex medical history. Again, there was no need for blood transfusion, the lump was benign, and I recovered very quickly.

By this time, as I traveled to Hopkins for my transplant evaluation, I had spent plenty of time in hospitals already. Doctors were repeatedly amazed at my body's resiliency despite all my medical complications. Still, it seemed to me, one would have to be pretty desperate to consciously and willingly plan to undergo surgery requiring a lengthy hospitalization.

Did I really want a liver transplant?

And what if something went wrong and I didn't survive? I couldn't imagine Steve's grief and feelings of abandonment.

The haunting melodic flute of Narada's "Earth Songs" seeped through my mind's rantings. Steve's tenor chant, "Hey-yah, hey-yah, hey-yah," joined the Native American vocals as skeletal trees whizzed by in the February landscape.

Interestingly, I was going to learn about liver transplant on February 17, my older brother's fifty-first birthday. Richard had played such a significant role in my life. As children, he was my playmate and guide. When we were teens, he was a hero to me—an adventurer, a football player, a creative genius. After I left Wheaton, he pulled me out of a deep depression by involving me in a theater production. In the fall of 1970, I took a job as payroll clerk in one of the last remaining cigar factories in York. I concentrated on earning money and deciding where my life should go from there. At least, I was out of my bedroom depression and interacting with people—all thanks to my brother, Richard. I was entering this possibility for a gift of life on the anniversary of the day that he first breathed life.

The skyline of Baltimore pierced my vision.

"We're almost there," Steve reached over and squeezed my hand.

Route 83 ends in Baltimore about five blocks from Johns Hopkins' Meyerhoff Physicians Building. We parked in the ample parking garage and walked over the busy sidewalk to the glassy four-story structure.

I knew I was entering a domain of serious medical research as we passed parents pushing their children in wheelchairs, a stylish young woman wearing nose tubing and carting an oxygen tank, along with her Jimmy Chou purse. Did I really need to keep this appointment?

Steve led me to the elevator which took us and a blue smocked nurse to the fourth floor. At last, we arrived at a waiting area where there were arranged the typical end tables layered with an array of magazines—*Woman's Day, Golf Digest, Time.* Across from the chairs and tables stood a counter and a sliding glass panel where we were greeted by a quietly smiling attendant, Lisa, by her nametag.

"Margaret Spiese for a one-thirty appointment with Dr. Diehl," I stammered while trying to look confident.

"Okay." Her smile and calming voice settled my anxiety a bit. "Your date of birth?" "Your address? Phone number? Emergency contact?" "Do you have your insurance cards with you?"

How quickly I learned these questions were routine as time after time, over the following years, I visited doctors or was admitted to hospitals.

"Thank you. You may have a seat. We'll be with you shortly."

It is difficult to concentrate on reading, whether the book you've brought with you or a recipe from Ladies Home Journal, when you are about to see a doctor who may set you on a life-changing path.

After a nurse did the preliminaries—weight, blood pressure, temperature—Steve and I were escorted into an examining room, one of five within a circular suite. We waited only a few moments before a young woman, probably thirty-sevenish, Caucasian with a blondish shoulder-length bob, entered the room. Without her white medical jacket and stethoscope, she could have been a school friend of my niece. She introduced herself as one of the doctors on Johns Hopkins' transplant team. This did not necessarily mean she would be performing the surgery when the time came, but she would follow my case until the transplant. Dr. Diehl asked why I thought I needed a liver transplant.

As I tried to swallow the glob of terror in my throat, I managed to choke out, "Well, my gastroenterologist tells me I am in end-stage liver disease. But really, myself, I feel I've lived a long and full life, much longer than I was ever expected to survive. My sister and brother have allowed me to be present at the birth of a nephew and a niece. I've written a play and performed it for well over three hundred people. I've been privileged to participate with my husband in staging my professor's poetry. I've acted and sung and generally enjoyed life. I'm not sure I should have a liver that could save someone else's life."

She smiled, adjusting her jacket. "You always have the option to say no, right up until you're in the operating room. But just think. You could live to see your niece and nephew grow into adulthood. I'm sure your husband would like to be with you a lot longer. Women these days live well into their eighties. If we can give you a new liver, you could live that long, too."

The plan was to continue to closely monitor the blood and to meet with Dr. Diehl approximately every six weeks. Depending on how I progressed.

Next stop, Dr. Nelson, psychiatrist. He interviewed me asking about my illness and how I had coped with it. Also, he had me explain how I felt about getting a new liver. It was difficult for me to fathom how someone who was just saying a forever goodbye to their mother, brother, sister, or son, could give consent for organ donation. For sure, if I received such a gift, I would take care of it as best I could.

I thought of my college years and all the opening night and after show parties when alcohol was no stranger. Like many, in my depression, I sought numbness in a gin and tonic buzz. I forgot about the fact that I was different when I partied with friends. I justified my careless behavior by thinking, *My liver is already shot. I may as well enjoy life as much as I can.*

In the past few months, however, since that day in Dr. Srour's office, I had not taken a sip of alcohol. As my focus shifted to maintaining what life I had left, it was not difficult to say "No, thanks," to an offer from friends for a glass of wine or to order a club soda rather than an alcoholic drink at a restaurant or bar. I needed to stay as healthy as I possibly could.

When our interview ended, Dr. Nelson shuffled me over to an intern or fellow for testing. He talked with Steve while I solved little puzzles, putting pegs in holes, one hand at a time, then simultaneously with both hands. The medical assistant placed a line drawing before me.

It appeared to be a simple sketch of a cruise ship close to a dock. After I studied it briefly, he replaced that drawing with another, similar but with some differences. He asked what was missing from this sketch that was in the first. Next, we did some word sequencing to see how well I could repeat what he had just listed.

Later, Steve explained that they needed a baseline to compare in case, in a few months, my mind may be affected by liver toxins. That was scary. However, only a few months of blood testing passed before I was indeed placed on a liquid, Lactulose. This substance catches excess ammonia released by a diseased liver before it can travel to the brain. I learned that we all need some ammonia in our systems, but too much can cause a brain dysfunction called *hepatic encephalopathy*. One can suffer memory loss, hallucination, or severe confusion. There are cases of HE where people have become extremely morose or even violent when ammonia levels are unchecked.

Life just holds so many surprises!

Our trip home was much chattier, as a lot of tension had been released.

"I can't wrap my mind around the possibility of living into my eighties!"

All my life I'd been given limits. First, the doctors told Mother and Daddy I wouldn't survive my first hospital stay at age thirteen. Then they said there was the slim chance I would live to graduate high school. After I surprised them by celebrating my eighteenth birthday, they predicted I wouldn't last beyond age twenty-one. By the time I shattered that prophecy, I had met Dr. Thorsen, a real gastroenterologist. When I asked him my prognosis, he thought there was no doubt I could reach age thirty-five. When I celebrated my thirty-fifth birthday, I made a conscious decision to never again ask a doctor what my life expectancy might be. I had already baffled them with my dogged determination. Besides that, who knew the true power of alpha waves, good energy, and prayer emanating from so many constant souls who surrounded me? I had learned to say thanks for each day. Still, I never took for granted or assumed I would be commemorating my next birthday. I basically took care of my chronic illness and focused on living.

So to think of surviving as long as eighty years, that that could be something I should expect, was unfathomable.

"How long did she say we might wait before I'm called?"

It was a good thing Steve was with me during the visit. My mind was so scattered as these life-altering possibilities were becoming reality, it seemed I could remember very little.

Steve pulled out into the speedy flow of traffic on Route 83 leaving Baltimore.

"She said as long as you are doing pretty well, you probably won't be called. The sickest people are highest on the list. It could be a year. It could be four years. We just have to wait and see."

After our hour and twenty minute drive, we were in front of our beautiful little brick home. Snow began falling, gently daubing the landscape in lacy silence.

CHAPTER 38

Productive Waiting

As a result of my evaluation that day in February, I was considered a viable candidate for liver transplant and placed on the UNOS (United Network for Organ Sharing) transplant list on May 14, 1998. My wait could be as short as two months or as long as five years (if I lived that long).

Dr. Diehl suggested I may wish to contact the American Liver Foundation (ALF). The nonprofit organization assists transplant patients in creating a fund to pay medical expenses. So I found ALF on the internet and downloaded the application form. After completing and mailing the necessary form, I was assigned an account number. ALF sent a booklet describing various methods to raise funds. I simply had to instruct contributors to indicate my account number on their check.

For someone in end-stage liver disease, such a task is very overwhelming. I was struggling to ramp up the energy to get through each day, much less concentrate on raising money.

As usual, my mother stepped up and told her beauty shop customers about the fund. My dear friend Alice held a yard sale with her little daughter, our godchild, at her side. All totaled, my mother and Alice raised approximately four thousand dollars.

The ALF booklet suggested that a fundraising committee be organized on behalf of the patient. At first, I was very skeptical about this. In a phone conversation with Alice, I told her, "ALF says we should create a fundraising organization. I'm not sure how to do that."

I could almost hear Alice's neurons popping.

"You have lots of friends and people who care about you. You just have to invite them to help."

"But, Alice, I can't ask for money for myself!"

Firmly, she stated, "Peggy, never deny people the opportunity to give."

And so it began.

As we considered who to enlist into the group, certain friends from my theater life came to mind. One man was an educator, very diplomatic, and a respected leader. Others were skilled in public relations; all of them were extremely creative. And above all, they were greatly concerned about me.

I thought of the various areas of my life. How could I reach the most people? Theater was the most active and present of my experiences. I was still on the membership roll and occasionally attended the little country church where I grew up. I had been active in the neighbors helping neighbors Society of Farm Women of Pennsylvania. And most recently, I was working part-time as typist and proofreader for Lancaster Newspapers. After selecting a few key friends from each of these areas, I thought of one or two other friends who had their own special skills and spheres of influence.

With advice and assistance from brother Richard and a lawyer friend, the little gathering of friends created *Garet's Hope*. These creative people held events including Basket Bingo, concerts, plays, participated in Lancaster County's bicycle fundraiser *Dream Ride,* and simply set out a jar on a counter for contributions.

Surely, this could be considered a dream fulfilled.

May 5, 1999—Moved to 2-B status.

I'm feeling great these days. Some weeks I work a lot at the newspaper—3–4 five-hour days and others I don't work at all like this week.

Visited my doctor at Johns Hopkins last Thursday. She says I'm pretty stable (not mentally—LOL), but I got some blood work done and she thinks I'll be upgraded to the next category (2-B). There are four categories: 1: You're critical, usually hospitalized, and may die any time without a new organ; 2-A: You're in intensive care and being helped by some machine or other; 2-B: You've been on the list a while, and your liver is degenerating—you're taking more and more medicine to keep you going; and 3: You're still responding well to drugs, are totally functional, and should be on the list for future safeguards.

Of course, all my theater friends are having a field day with this: 2-B or not 2-B, as in Shakespeare's Hamlet.

Well, it's hard to believe, but I've been on the list for a year this month! And since I've been battling this condition since age thirteen, my liver is finally wearing out. (She says that's why the high fluctuating blood sugars). But in my opinion, I've truly been blessed with prayers and good medical care…hardly anyone even knew I was ill until I announced I was on the transplant list! And I'm still the healthiest sick person I know.

So the doctors say I'm a survivor—people usually last 10 years max with this condition—I've had it for thirty-five years! And so I'm a great transplant candidate. If possible, they'd like to do it while I'm still healthy. Actually, it will take me a while to get used to the idea (I can't imagine putting myself in the hospital willfully!). And there's so much I want to do before (and after). I've formed this terrific fundraising committee, and we have high hopes of raising the twenty-one to twenty-five thousand dollars per year to pay for drugs for twenty years following the

179

operation. It will give us such a wonderful opportunity to educate people about organ transplantation and the great shortage of organs, simply because even if you put donation on your driver's license, you need to talk with family about your wishes because, in the end, they make the decision. And giving is such a healing blessing.

So that's how I am, and life is succulent—especially this time of year. I LOVE SPRING! And after transplant, you're not allowed to dig in the garden for a year—so I have to plant as many perennials as I can now!

CHAPTER 39

Impediment

In late May 1999, I developed a little water blister, about the size of a dime, on my lower right leg, approaching the ankle. This was routine for me as, in spite of taking diuretics, I regularly experienced edema in my legs due to prednisone intake. The condition was especially aggravated when I was unable to elevate my legs due to a busy schedule. But I had to keep on living! I couldn't just stay at home in bed or in a reclining chair all day long.

What's more, with the overt pronouncement by several doctors that I was now in end-stage organ failure, I wanted to cram as much living as possible into the time I had left. For the past year, not only was I working about twenty to thirty hours a week for CoMotion, a small improv theater, as public relations associate, I had also taken the job as proofreader and typist three days a week at Lancaster Newspapers. Additionally, I volunteered as usher, property mistress, house manager, or hairstylist for a couple other theaters in town. I guess it was inevitable that I blew a gasket with that schedule and a failing liver.

I had gotten little water blisters like this before. I treated them by keeping the area clean and covering the blister with a Band-Aid. After a day or so, the blister would drain. Then, I put on the opening a bit of antibiotic ointment and a sprinkle of powdered golden seal. Within three or four days, the opening would be healed.

My body has always been slow to heal, yet another side effect of prednisone. Then in 1985, after a series of vaginal infections, when I visited the gynecologist, I was diagnosed with diabetes mellitus type II. This, apparently, was no surprise to my gastroenterologist. Even patients who take a five-day course of prednisone for a case of poison ivy are warned that the drug may elevate their blood sugar.

Amazingly, the general practitioner I had visited for that series of vaginal yeast infections, knowing that I had taken the steroid for twenty years, never checked me for diabetes. Instead, he treated the symptoms with a prescription fungicide.

Diabetes added a whole new dimension to my medical life. Blood glucose testing three to four times a day and yet another oral medication became part of my routine.

I researched how to take care of diabetes, what I could do to minimize its effects. In all my reading, the first suggestion was to lose weight. At five foot, three inches, I weighed 125 pounds. No. This did not apply to me.

It took me several months to work through the denial stage most newly diagnosed diabetics feel. But soon, I adjusted my diet, learned to control my sweet tooth, and pretty much integrated taking care of the diabetes into my already subnormal life.

Diabetes, however, is notorious for delaying healing by destroying the circulatory system. This is why so many diabetics experience amputations.

The tiny dime-sized blister refused to heal. I gave it my regular cleansing, antibiotic salve, and golden seal treatment. But the opening didn't heal. It bled and formed a scab which became inflamed. After a few days, the leg hurt so badly I could not walk on it.

My general practitioner prescribed antibiotics. If there was no improvement within three days, I was instructed to call for another appointment.

The pain increased. That very weekend at the end of May 1999, Johns Hopkins transplant center held a one-day transplant seminar in Towson, Maryland. Sessions on taking care of the waiting transplant candidate, how to stay healthy in preparation for transplant, taking care of the caregiver, financial concerns in the transplant process, and new developments in transplantation were slated for presentation.

Since prior to this blister problem, I had already registered husband Steve, Mother and Daddy, and me to attend, we rented a wheelchair for me and drove to the Marriott in Towson. Although I was distracted by the pain in my leg, the sessions were informative. At lunch, we ate with a family who had experienced the waiting and finally got the call that saved the father's life. We also learned that day that Johns Hopkins had performed their first living donor liver transplant in October 1998. When my mother heard that a donated partial liver can regenerate in a recipient within a few months, she was ready to jump up on the operating table to give part of her own liver to save my life. At age seventy-six, there may have been health conditions that would prohibit her donation. But the very knowledge of this new possibility raised her hopes. She was never tested as a potential donor. After we shared this information with the family, I believe my brother, Tim, went through some of the preliminary testing. However, we subsequently learned that, in these early stages of surgical research, adult partial liver donations were given only to children and infants.

Although the day was stimulating, I was happy to arrive back home where I could suffer in peace. By the next day, the pain was unbearable. When Tuesday morning arrived, I could suffer no longer. The dime-sized blister had expanded to the size of a golf ball and looked very dark. I phoned the doctor's office.

"Dr. Jafri told me to make another appointment if my leg hadn't improved in three days, so I'm calling to schedule."

"We can see you Thursday at 2 p.m.," the saccharin voice replied.

"No. That is not suitable. I need to see someone today. My leg is turning black!"

"Oh. Dr. Jafri may be able to squeeze you in at 1 p.m. today."

"I'll be there. Thank you."

I did not return home from my appointment that day. Tuesday, June 1, 1999, was the beginning of my horrific experience. Bacteria had taken up residence under the blister's scab and were munching away and killing healthy tissue.

Dr. Jafri admits me to Columbia Hospital. There is talk of amputation. But Dr. Jafri fights for me, suggesting a course of hyperbaric oxygenation therapy, a relatively experimental procedure. (This won't happen until I leave the hospital.) After a few days, I am admitted to Lancaster General Hospital where wound doctors begin to study my case. The second day there, I am taken downstairs to a place where my lower leg is submerged in a whirlpool to soften the tissue. Then, while I sit in a chair with the leg somewhat elevated so the doctor can get to it, he slowly and gently clips away at the dead tissue.

Since I am in great pain, I am administered oxycodone at regular intervals. My first experience with narcotics, I become very depressed and emotionally vulnerable. The drug gives me relief from the pain for about two hours. Recommended administration is every six hours.

Under these circumstances, I return to my room after a visit to the whirlpool area. I am back perhaps an hour and a half when Dr. Schmidt enters.

"I understand you have a little boo-boo on your leg."

He unceremoniously tears back the sheet. Without asking, he removes the dressing that had been applied down in the whirlpool room.

"Nurse, get me a sutures kit."

Taking the scissors from the kit, he proceeds to snip away at my leg.

I grit my teeth and try to breathe through the agony.

"I hear you're waiting for a liver transplant. They don't always work, you know."

Chop. Chop. Chop. Chop.

Finally, I beg, "Enough! Please stop!"

Chop. Chop. Snip. Snip.

Finally, after interminable torture, he leers. "Okay. I guess I'll let you go now. This doesn't look good." And he leaves the room as abruptly as he arrived.

Nurses immediately comfort me as I sob and sob.

Is it true my newest dream of liver transplant will be squelched?

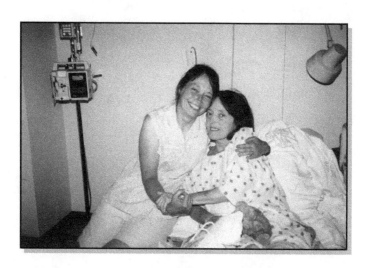

Ever-supportive Kathy
Lancaster General Hospital June 1999

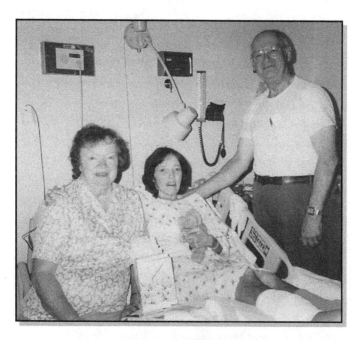

Angels all around
Mother and Daddy
Cards and Teddy Bear Scrumpy

CHAPTER 40

Last Days

Tuesday, May 23, 2000

In order to qualify, the patient must have undergone certain serious medical crises and their liver function tests must manifest abnormalities within a certain range.

I was told I may live until age twenty-one. When I began applying to university, Mother asked the doctors if she should allow me to go to college. Their reply, "Let her live as normal a life as possible." In college, the fluid retention increased, the hemorrhaging episodes began and the prognosis was maybe age twenty-six. Steve and I were married in 1974 at age twenty-four. My best friend told me, "Now your health is getting better because you have something to live for!" My brothers helped me escape the "glass house" I was living in—restricting myself from autumn hikes through woods and fields, swimming, and other "strenuous" activities. Steve got me to the gym. My attitude became more focused on living life than worrying about losing life. Besides all this, I was supported in thoughts, prayers, and encouragement from wonderful friends, acquaintances, family, and even strangers who heard about me through others.

So now, my body is reaching end-stage liver disease where it is sucking off all my other life systems in order to keep the organism functioning. My case is extremely unusual in that people usually become very ill and face certain death immediately. Although that was the case with me in 1964, a collection of inexplicable forces and my own stubbornness gave me this life extension. And now, the gift of possibility in transplant. I was placed on the United Network for Organ Sharing (UNOS) transplant list on May 14, 1998.

I formed a fundraising committee, Garet's Hope, and in turn, we formed a foundation to benefit liver transplant candidates who have autoimmune hepatitis (Red Rose Autoimmune Hepatitis Liver Foundation— RRALF). Individuals and groups may give. Individuals and groups may perform their own fundraising events to benefit RRALF, or my account with the American Liver Foundation (ALF), or write checks directly to me. RRALF & ALF donations are tax-deductible, them both being 501(c)3 nonprofits. RRALF earns interest which can be funneled back into further fundraising; ALF reserves contributions for immediate medical costs to me and uses interest for administrative overhead and research and raising public awareness.

Right now, I am recuperating from a staphylococcus infection that all but destroyed my lower right leg in June 1999. However, since the infection had not reached the bone, amputation was set aside to see how healing progressed after extensive debridement (removal of dead tissue).

Doctors have replaced the glucose medication I was taking orally with a regimen of insulin. The insulin more tightly controls sugar levels which, when too high, impede healing. Now, the wound that had measured 8 1/2 by 7-1/4 inches and 2-1/4 inches deep has healed to normal skin level and measures about 3 by 4 inches. Additionally, I have been treated extensively with Hyperbaric Oxygenation Therapy. How fortunate we are that one of the few centers for this therapy is located right here in Columbia, Pennsylvania. Of course, I have the best caregiver in Stephen—researching and using herbs and giving me a strictly regimented diet, plus just the healing energy from his being. Friends have inundated me with loving, healing energy, and by new year, I will be dancing the night away.

Only good can come to those on the lookout for it.

Sunday, January 16, 2000

If and when I do get that telephone call that a liver is available for me, someone else will be in great agony. A wife will have lost her husband or a mother, her child. A sister may survive an accident and her brother may die.

How difficult it will be for someone to say, "Okay, he will never have his own heart beat again. Doctor, you may stop the ventilator so that someone else will live."

This is the person they met perhaps at school. They fell in love, flirted with, and courted one another's hearts. They won each other's love and had a wedding and a romantic honeymoon. Perhaps babies were born. They shared secrets and fears and bought each other tokens of love on Valentine's Day. They kissed under the mistletoe and when the New Year came in.

Whether their time together was short or long, it was rich. Not something to enjoy, toss the packaging, and get another.

Someone with this history and deep feelings will have to say, "Yes, you may end this life so another's will be extended."

Can I accept such a gift? Put someone in that position? Am I worth such travail and precise expertise?

My friend, Lou, says that perhaps whoever becomes my donor was placed on this Earth precisely for that purpose. That we are already cosmically connected. If that is the case, I am praying for that person even now…that they will live life to the fullest, cherish each day, tell those they love how much they love them. Until we are one.

Sunday a.m., June 11, 2000

Finally, last night, I received the phone call we've been fantasizing about these many months.

She would not talk to Steve, but insisted she must speak with me.

"Margaret, this is Cindy Cohen from Johns Hopkins. We have a local donor and your name came up."

However, I still have this large open wound in my leg and am taking antibiotics for cellulitis in the same leg.

So she said she would page the surgeon and tell him these things to get his response. Then she would call back.

When we talked again after twenty minutes, she said Dr. Markowitz can't transplant someone with an open wound.

So now, I know I won't be called until my skin graft is done, and I'm healed up from that. But the phone call brought many thoughts. Someone else is having difficulty sleeping tonight because they had to say goodbye to someone they loved very dearly.

Who was that person? How did they die? Were the survivors deciding then and there what to give, if anything? Dear Lord, be with them, give them peace, bring them a sense of satisfaction in their generosity.

If I had been able to undergo the operation, I would probably be being prepped right now. Hopefully, someone else is.

And Steve is very motivated now to get things in order—to be knowledgeable about our steps from admission through ICU. He wants to call our lawyer Bill Haynes and get in there to finalize a will.

I want to have contact lists well-defined.

And insurance taken care of.

And my desk/office/house in order.

So when it is time, all I need concentrate on is getting better.

But as for now, I remain on the journey. Funny how I may have to add a new segment to my life. It's always been:

Before I was sick.

While I was sick (After I got sick).

Soon I will add: Post transplant (When I was no longer sick)

Now, however, I must get this leg healed. And there are other things to keep me occupied.

I just hope, when the call comes, I can be filled with peace…and the world has enough space for my JOY!

Waiting for the Call, 2000

CHAPTER 41

Dry Run

The leg wound was healing in stages. Dr. Michael Flood had treated me weekly since June 1999. Besides routine debridement, he performed Apligraf surgery and, at another time, a skin graft using a donation from my thigh, requiring yet another hospitalization. Steve changed dressings daily. Cautiously, I was able to ride in the car and walk short distances.

I had been very disappointed that the first call for transplant from Hopkins was taken off the table by the surgeon because of the leg wound. It was taking forever to heal. If my wound had to be closed before doctors would perform the transplant, I wasn't sure my body could last long enough.

Then, on Saturday, July 8, 2000, the phone rang.

"This is Cindy, transplant coordinator at Johns Hopkins. We have a liver for you if you want it."

"I still have a wound in my leg. Is that okay?"

"Are you on antibiotics?"

"No. But I thought…"

"This doctor says as long as there is no infection, he would like to give you the transplant. Just go to the ER and tell them why you are there."

Our hearts in our throats, Steve and I notified our families that we were on our way to Baltimore. The big day had arrived.

In the ER, after I was dressed in a hospital gown, a nurse came to me with a bottle of iodine and some sterile cloths. She told me to swab my entire abdomen in the solution. After performing this frightening preparation, I lay back on the gurney in the tiny cubicle. Steve was patiently waiting beside me as a phlebotomist inserted an IV in my arm. She used the IV site to draw blood for various tests. Moments later, Mother and Daddy and Kathy arrived.

As we spoke, I felt like I was on my deathbed saying goodbye.

After a brief wait, I was taken to a regular hospital room. My family was permitted to stay with me. Their presence reassured me. I needed to be grounded at this time when my entire body was chilled with nervous anticipation.

A nurse came to take my vitals. Blood pressure. Temperature. Pulse rate. Everything looked good, he said.

Then, a few moments later, he came back with a bag of fluid.

"Your potassium is a bit low. We will give you some through your IV. Let's see. It is now 6 p.m. The surgeon would like you in surgery by seven o'clock, so we'll do this quickly."

Potassium is a salt. We all know how painful it is to get salt in a wound. Imagine salt flowing rapidly into your veins. It was excruciating. As the potassium raced into my vein, I moaned and grit my teeth. Steve gently encouraged me to say, "Thank you, more."

Twenty minutes later, when the fluid was almost into me, a surgeon came into the room.

"You can get dressed and go home. We found a hepatitis antigen in the donated liver, so we can't transplant it. Sorry. I guess you can call this a dry-run."

So we all got ready to go home. I remember, as we walked through the hospital toward the parking garage, I saw people with Igloo coolers coming inside. I wondered if there could be a donated organ in one of those coolers, an organ that would indeed save someone's life that very evening.

CHAPTER 42

Learning Acceptance

Friday, September 29, 2000

Supposedly, we are on the verge of a new and better life. More accurately, I would say simply, a whole new life— with new challenges and many unchanged. Still learning patience and tolerance and various ways of loving one another and taking care of one another.

They say I need a new and healthier liver. But right now, my heart is breaking. I don't have the knowledge or energy to help Steve through these stressful days. He is working hard to make money for us to pay for the house and the car and all the amenities of living a far from prosperous life. He works hard to maintain the house with what few resources we have. He fixes and creates and still finds time to serve others in song and theater technique. He takes care that I am fed healthful, life-giving foods and nutrients. He encourages me to exercise and rest, be productive, and think positively. He has worked magic on my wounded leg so that what was once a 4×5 inch, 1-1/2 inch deep hole is now completely filled in and nearly fully healed.

And yet I cannot love him enough or properly. The stress and terrorizing anticipation of transplant makes me irritable and sleepless. I pretend to be handling it well. "Day by day," I tell people. It's all any of us have. But I think I would prefer to live life without the hope of extended life dangling before me.

It's like someone is about to offer me a million dollars. I'd better dang well do something responsible with it or wallow in guilt for the remainder of my days if I waste even a penny!

So if you think I need a new liver, you'd better give me a stronger heart right along with it!

Thank you.

Surrounded by Love
Summer 2000

Late April 2001

DREAM

*D*arkness. Cool. Smells damp, like church camp. Silence. Utter silence. I step tentatively to advance, where? I don't know. Out of the darkness.

But then, does my hope make it so? There is enough light that I see I am in a cave. The roughened walls shimmer with moisture. A stream runs swiftly paralleling my path to the right.

As I step along, now with a bit more assurance, the rock wall to my left develops a shelf. I use the wall as a guide as I inch my way forward.

The trickle of the stream provides a sense of life to my uncertain trek. Then, I hear an added sound, the high chirp of a bird. There, on the rock wall shelf, highlighted by an eerie glow, hops a bright red cardinal.

It does not flutter away from me, but seems to coax me to follow it. And so, obeying instincts beyond reason, I do just that. The cardinal seems to be privy to wisdom I lack.

As I abandon my trepidation to this tiny creature of loveliness, it takes flight, leading me forward to a bright opening of the cave.

Sunshine swathes the green meadow before me as the cardinal flies off to light in a nearby dogwood, donned in white blossoms. Scent of greening leaves washes over me. My heart swells with joy, confidence, and gratitude.

And I awaken.

CHAPTER 43

An Offer of New Life

Ring! Rrriinnngg!

The phone startles me awake. Is Mother calling to invite us to dinner? I wonder through the grog of sleep. I fumble for the cordless phone we have kept on the bedstand in case of a call from Baltimore.

"Hello?"

"Hello. This is Cathy, the transplant coordinator from Johns Hopkins."

Suddenly, I am fully awake and sitting up in bed. My stomach flutters inside, and I reach to nudge Steve sleeping next to me as I reply,

"Yes, good morning."

Could this be the call we've been anticipating or just another false alarm? Would I be awaking in this, my own, room tomorrow morning?

"We have a donor liver that matches you. It is from a seventeen-year-old girl. We would like you to measure your girth around the abdomen. Can you do that?"

Stunned, I answer, "Surely."

"I'll phone you again in about five minutes."

"Okay." I numbly place the phone back on the bedstand.

Sheets rustle as Steve rolls toward me and reaches out to stroke my back.

"What was that all about?"

"Johns Hopkins. This could be it. I'm supposed to measure my gut."

I stumble to the next room. The beautiful quilt-topped sewing box Steve gave me last Christmas sits primly beside my antique treadle Singer sewing machine.

"Will I soon have energy to make skirts and dresses and fun hats in this room?" I wonder as I rifle through the box, looking for my tape measure.

Hands shaking, I find it and wrap the red cloth tape around my rib cage. But my eyes cannot focus on the white lines between the numbers.

"Steve, could you please help me read this?"

He had snuggled into the pillow again for a few last dreams.

"Huh? Oh. Sure. Come 'ere, babe."

I fight back tears as his legs slide over the side of the bed and he sits up. The sun streams through the window, gilding flowered sheets and worn wooden floor. Dust particles glint on the dresser.

"Twenty-eight and three-quarter inches," Steve measures. He encircles me with his arms and pulls me close. His head against my bosom, he continues, "and I love every inch!"

The phone rings. I report our findings.

"One moment please. I'll check with my husband." I place my hand over the mouthpiece. Then, to Steve, "This is it. How soon can we get to Hopkins?"

Now fully awake, he asks, "What time is it now? Oh. Never mind. Ask if noon is soon enough."

After I push the button to disconnect the call, I stare at the phone. Steve's voice disturbs my suspended moment.

"Well?" Steve asks.

"Uh. Sure. Yes. Noon is okay."

And I feel nauseous. Like the many times just before stepping onstage or making a speech in school or just before an unfamiliar medical procedure. My eyes well up with unexpected tears.

"What time is it now?" I choke.

Steve lays his hand on my shoulder. "It's 8:40 by this clock. It takes about an hour and forty minutes to get to Baltimore. We should leave in maybe an hour and a half or forty-five."

An hour and a half!

Thoughts tumble over one another racing through my head.

I need to dress, to pack. But what? I was told to bring nothing. But I have to have writing material and something to read and—pictures! Where are my photos of my nieces and nephews? And my little teddy bear, Scrumpy? I should phone people. Get my phone chain started. I need my friends praying for me and the doctors, sending positive energy through the universe during the operation.

The operation.

As I pull off my nightgown, I stand before the mirror and stroke my bare abdomen. I will never see it smooth and unscarred after today. Is this really what I want? Is this the right thing to do? I have already lived so long and so well, even with all the ups and downs of looming terminal illness. Should I not just allow nature to take its course? To take me from this plane of living?

Steve's voice jolts me back to the sun swathed bedroom. "I'll get some coffee going…What would you like…can you have any breakfast?"

"I'll just munch on a granola bar in the car."

My eyes drink in every detail surrounding me. My gaze falls on our lovely calico cat perched on the windowsill. Her patchy coat gleams in the morning sunshine.

In the kitchen, Steve rattles Iams out of the bag and into the cat's dish.

"Maybe you should call your brother, Rich. I'll call Mom, but she's probably in church."

"Yeah. Everybody is," I echo.

Everything seems unreal, distant, happening in slow motion. I inhale deeply and concentrate on breathing slowly.

"I'll find the church directory for Mount Zion Church. That will take care of Mother and Daddy and brother Tim's family. I'll try Kathy and Rich when we're in the car."

Gee. I guess I'll have to return this pager now…or sometime soon. Breathe. Don't get ahead of yourself.

Oh no. I wanted to wash the kitchen floor. And how did all these books pile up here beside my reading chair? Do I need to take my medicine with me? I guess we really ought to eat something more than granola bars. Or should I before surgery? Should I take my morning insulin? Oh. This is just too complicated. Too inconvenient. Do I really want to go through with this? I need to touch Steve and my gorgeous soft cat. I need to lock in the sight of my cozy little house—the bricked fireplace, the mantel laden with jade plant, a dull finished brass bugle and mosaic plate inlaid with white, yellow, blue, and red tiles to form the loaves and fishes spoken of in the Bible. A gift from sister-in-law Suanne at Christmastime with a note attached to the back, "Miracles still happen today."

True. So true. A miracle is happening right now. Amidst all of the uncertainty and anticipation speeding through me at this moment, way down deep there runs a constant current of assurance. I am cared for here and now. A Greater Power is conducting this symphony of events. A breath of Peace.

"Are you ready?" Steve asks cheerfully, keys in one hand, backpack in the other.

"Never." I smile. I embrace him and lay my lips on his in a soft lingering kiss. Then, cuddling into his shoulder. "We're stepping into a new life."

CHAPTER 44

Receiving the Gift

The drive to Baltimore is a long and skin-prickling interlude as both of us anticipate, we know not what. New possibilities? Loss? Gain? Life? We are stepping into a space vehicle for a journey somewhere we've never been.

I make phone calls to some key people. They are all in church and Sunday school. Brian answers at Middletown and says he will go to the church to tell Rich and Su. Later, I learned he entered the Sanctuary just as Pastor Su asked for Praise and Prayer Concerns. So he announced I was on my way. At Mount Zion Church, I speak to brother Tim, tell him what is happening, then he finds Mother and puts her on the phone. I wish her Happy Mother's day, hoping she can accept this transplant as her gift. I call sister Kathy's cell phone and leave a message on her voice mail. Again, later, I learned that Rich phoned Kathy and Russ as they arrived home from church. Kathy phones us just as we are driving off of I83 onto Fayette Avenue in downtown Baltimore, three blocks from Johns Hopkins University Medical Center.

From there, we enter Johns Hopkins' emergency system. I am wheeled here and there. The efficiency of everyone is so calmly hurried that a mist of excited anticipation coats every movement. I am taken to a prep/examination area where I sign papers stating that I understand the risks surrounding this surgery. There are other papers to sign: releases to insurance and consent to treatment papers, all while I am being attached to a heart monitor and having an IV started. The young dark-skinned man in the curtained unit opposite me has a kidney problem. I believe he is a former transplant because he seems to know the personnel from past visits. His attitude is light and humorous.

Steve stays right with me through all of this. We talk a little bit about basketball as the NBA playoffs are in full swing: the Milwaukee Bucks, the Philadelphia '76ers, the Los Angeles Lakers, and San Antonio Spurs. Our nurse is a cute little dark-skinned lady who enjoys Molly Sweeney from *Saturday Night Live*. She does some imitations of Sweeney characters and says her sister thinks she's crazy when she does this. Her sis doesn't watch SNL.

Surgery is scheduled for 5:00 p.m. So after a while (I keep asking "what time is it?" trying to remain calm. But the butterflies in my stomach are unbelievable), a troop of hospital-garbed folks come and wheel my gurney away. But not before I bid Steve goodbye with lingering looks and kisses and hand holding I dread letting go.

The ride through the hospital corridor is long and spooky. As one young female doctor tells me, "We're taking you through the bowels of the hospital."

We move over bumpy floors, past roughly plastered walls and pipe-mazed ceilings, and then just seem to stop. There, outside some windowed doors, which I presume to be the OR, we are joined by a few more doctors, male and female, very young—most likely students. They introduce themselves to me.

Obviously, this is a big event!

Then, one young lady in scrubs smiles. "We understand you'd like a little relaxer before we go inside."

Gratefully and nervously I answer, "Yes. That would be a good thing."

In previous visits I confessed to Dr. Diehl that I have had visions of freaking out at the last minute, changing my mind about having the operation, and leaping off the table. But before long, someone injects the sleepy fluid into the IV. I quickly thank them all for being here for me. I never see the operating room or the surgeons.

Through the darkness, I hear a tender, familiar voice, the voice I have heard since my first awakening from the darkness of the womb.

"Peggy…we're right here with you."

My eyes fly open.

I learn, much later, that I have startled my fourteen-year-old nephew, Isaac, who jumps a few steps back, away from the foot of the bed. Apparently, the family, who had waited and prayed throughout the long night (a short eight hours for a liver transplant) in the surgical waiting room, did not expect any reaction from my anesthetized body. In fact, they were simply looking upon my bloated, IV-impacted, quietly still body, with silent concern, when the attending doctor exclaimed, "Go on, you can touch her! She won't break!"

So Mother takes my hand and calls my name, "Peggy…"

Through a dreamlike haze, I see them all. Surrounding my bed. My drugged mind cannot be specific. But I am immersed in love…it is all I need…exactly what I need in this moment.

The kind voice continues, "You don't need to say anything. We are here with you. You are doing just fine. We love you."

Does a tear drop on me? Is it my own? Does it fall from an angel?

At peace, I slip back into a deep sleep.

A DREAM

I am in a very foreign setting. Unlike my Pennsylvania home of oak and maple and dogwood trees, this land is overgrown with tall, broad-leafed jungle foliage. As I struggle to move forward on a nonexistent path, I am strangled on every side with tangled brush. A cacophony of insects of every sort agitates the air.

Gasping, at last I come to an open field. Perhaps I can escape to familiar surroundings. But as I race out into the expanse, bright electric sparks arise sporadically from the ground to torture each step. The flashes threaten pain of shock and trauma.

Suddenly, I am being pursued by scantily clothed black men, donned with bone necklaces and nose piercings. They flail spears as they run toward me. I cannot escape them.

Certain they are about to skin me alive, I scream out,

And awaken in my hospital bed, morphine racing through my veins.

CHAPTER 45

A Difference

The first few days following the transplant, I was in surgical intensive care, SICU in hospital speak. I had a central line in my neck, at least three drains in my lower abdomen, a chevron of seemingly countless staples on my abdomen where my liver had been removed and a healthy liver implanted, a catheter, and an IV site. Nurses turning me in the bed was a major event.

To perform most any surgery, it is necessary to pump the patient with extra air and fluid to provide working space. For a major surgery like my liver transplant, it seemed to me they had used gallons of water! At least, that's how I felt. I was extremely bloated. Large doses of morphine made the world unreal. I was constantly in and out of consciousness.

The stomach's automatic response to process food and fluids is called peristalsis. My peristalsis was inactive due to residual effects of anesthesia, so my stomach would have filled with anything I ingested. If I vomited, the surgeons' carefully placed stitches may have ruptured resulting in internal hemorrhage. I was forbidden to drink even a sip of water, and I felt so thirsty. I was consumed with the desire for a tall glass of ice water.

When I was finally moved to regular ICU after several days, the central line was removed and I was taking fewer pain medications. Steve asked, "Do you feel any different than before the surgery?"

In spite of all my appliances, drains, IV, and catheter, I smiled. "For the first time I can remember, my blood feels clean!"

I did not know who was responsible for my second chance at life. Steve had been told only that my donor was a seventeen-year-old girl from Frederick, Maryland. He was also informed that the liver needed to be sutured a bit before transplant due to a tear, probably caused by a broken rib when CPR was performed.

In spite of the misery of those initial days, I was inexpressibly grateful and very mindful that someone had made the unselfish decision to donate their loved one's liver. I named my new organ "Grace." Truly, this gift in the family's hour of deepest grief was an act of grace, an unmerited gift.

Not until many months later, when I made contact with my donor's mother, did I learn their story of donation. A year before, Shelley had gone to the Maryland DMV with her dad to test for her driver's license. On the form was the question, "Do you wish to indicate you are an organ donor?" Confused by this question, she asked her dad what "organ donor" meant. He briefly explained to her that, should she ever be in an accident and die, her organs could be used to save someone very ill.

"But you don't have to worry about that, sugar."

Being the giving person she was, Shelley asked for his approval to check the organ donor box. She passed her test, became a licensed driver, and organ donation became an afterthought.

A little more than twelve months passed, when Shelley was lying in a hospital bed, her life supported by medical equipment. When her parents saw her driver's license, they were reminded of her selfless decision to be an organ donor. According to her mother, Shelley was a giver and a savior. She brought home helpless animals and always gave whatever any of her friends needed. Their love for her prompted her grieving parents to consent to donation. Shelley saved my life and the lives of several others through this immeasurable gift of life.

I continued to communicate via letters and e-mail with Shelley's mother for several years. She confided in me that she was grateful to know I was doing well, that Shelley's gift was truly helping me. I can never thank her sufficiently.

CHAPTER 46

Forever in Light

The sojourn in the hospital was like being born all over again. I had to regain trust in my ability to help myself. To say I felt vulnerable would be an understatement. So intense was my fright that I did not want to have a bowel movement for fear I would leave my new liver in the toilet. For some reason, the stitches in one of the drains in my abdomen repeatedly tore open. As a result, fluid leaked out and my hospital gown became soaked. The air-conditioning on the wet gown was so cold!

One morning, I awoke to find myself drenched. My impulse was to cry. When I found myself in tears, calling for help, I actually interrupted myself.

"I don't need help. I can do this myself."

I got up out of the bed, trailing my IV pole with me to the bathroom, where I found a towel to dry myself. When I returned to the bed, I hit the call button for the nurse to bring me a dry gown. She also changed the wet sheets. Before long, another troupe of interns arrived. As I lay in the bed watching and listening to James Taylor on the *Today Show*, on the phone with Steve so we could enjoy "You've Got a Friend" together, the doctors stitched me back together again.

About seven days after transplant, I was gurnied downstairs through the depths of Johns Hopkins to nuclear medicine. There they placed me in the dark, under a huge machine, for what seemed an interminable period. I was nothing less than terrified. What if this great thing gave way and crushed me? I buried my tears in the soft plush dog nephew Brian had brought to me in the early SICU days. I felt so alone, so cold, so desperate. Finally, I was returned to my room. There I shivered and trembled in fear and desperation, wondering how I would ever get through all of this.

A knock came at my door. In walked my mother and father and beautiful sister. Kathy handed to me a little decorated cardboard plaque, pink framed with bees and butterflies and flowers all around, which my dear niece, Amy, had made especially for me. On it was Psalm 139 (NIV).

> [1] You have searched me, LORD,
>   and you know me.
> [2] You know when I sit and when I rise;
>   you perceive my thoughts from afar.
> [3] You discern my going out and my lying down;
>   you are familiar with all my ways.
> [4] Before a word is on my tongue
>   you, LORD, know it completely.
> [5] You hem me in behind and before,
>   and you lay your hand upon me.
> [6] Such knowledge is too wonderful for me,
>   too lofty for me to attain.
> [7] Where can I go from your Spirit?
>   Where can I flee from your presence?
> [8] If I go up to the heavens, you are there;
>   if I make my bed in the depths, you are there.
> [9] If I rise on the wings of the dawn,
>   if I settle on the far side of the sea,
> [10] even there your hand will guide me,
>   your right hand will hold me fast.
> [11] If I say, "Surely the darkness will hide me
>   and the light become night around me,"

¹² even the darkness will not be dark to you;
    the night will shine like the day,
    for darkness is as light to you.

We read the Psalm aloud together. Comforting me to my very soul. I told them about the frightening experience in the darkness of nuclear medicine. Their timing was perfect.

Then, a nurse walked in and said, "The pictures weren't right. We need to take you downstairs again."

This time, Mother and Daddy and Kathy went with me. I was still frightened, but kept clinging to these promises, that I was seen even in what was darkness to me. "For darkness is as light to (the Great Source)."

So as this Psalm touched me then, I share it with you now, hoping you may find light where there is darkness and know that you are never alone.

Supporters:
Niece Charity, Nephew Isaac, Niece Amy, Brother Tim
Johns Hopkins 2001

AFTERWORD

The first year after transplant was a series of nightmares. My regular regimen of medications was increased. I had to take two immunosuppressants (anti-rejection drugs) several times each day: Cellcept and Prograf. Additionally, I had to take prednisone, Lasix, Protonix, and the anti-fungal Mycelex. The schedule was 8 a.m., 10 a.m., noon, 2 p.m., 4 p.m., 8 p.m., and 10 p.m. The problem was that I could barely swallow. Following the operation, when I finally graduated after three or four days from IV nutrition and Jell-O to regular meals, I found I could not ingest the food easily. I took a bite and chewed and chewed, but could not get it down. When she visited me at mealtime, my mother, as mothers do, urged me to try to eat at least half of my chicken salad sandwich. Although I desperately wanted to, it was impossible for me to do. Alice, always compassionate, understanding, and affirming, came to visit; she wrote in my journal, "Today, Peggy has been in the hospital five days; today, she took five bites. Tomorrow, she will be in the hospital six days; tomorrow, she will take six bites."

Although Alice's advice to take baby steps encouraged me and took the pressure off, I continued to wrestle with swallowing. I dreaded pill time because I knew I faced an hour of choking and drowning in sips of water.

This was so depressing I cried over my food and blinked back tears as the nurse entered my room with her pharmacy cart. I knew that, in order to gain strength and to protect my new liver, I needed to take these pills and to eat. But it just wasn't working.

After fourteen days in the hospital, I was discharged. At home, I continued to struggle with downing pills and food. The problem was finally addressed at a weekly follow-up appointment at Hopkins. The doctor explained that my esophageal opening was possibly bumped and bruised when I was intubated for the transplant. The problem resolved itself after approximately a month and a half.

I went to JHU for my transplant weighing 125 pounds. When I came home two weeks later, I weighed 145 pounds. Because of this major surgery, I had been pumped with fluid to make organs more accessible. While in surgical ICU, through my stupor, I heard a doctor sternly tell interns it was their assignment to double the amount of my fluid output by the next day at the same time. I repeatedly told visitors, "I'm so swollen, I feel like a tick!"

When I returned home, Steve faced the constant battle of arranging and rearranging pillows to support my puffy body. When he finally put me to bed at night and had a chance for time for himself, I called out, "Steve, can you help me turn? I can't breathe."

It took time and patience on both our parts, but the fluid slowly decreased and I became more comfortable and less afraid. By September, I felt almost like a normal person. I had so much energy that my morning would be filled with activity, making breakfast, washing dishes, dusting furniture. By eleven o'clock, I was exhausted.

"Oh no! I've played myself out!"

And I collapsed in the recliner. To my delight, after five minutes of rest, I was ready to go again. I had never before realized how much effort I needed to expend, prior to the transplant, simply to get out of bed, prepare for the day, and then do whatever I had to do.

I am still far from normal. However, after so many years of wishing for normality, I have learned to be content. An incredible fifteen years following transplant, I have been in and out of the hospital innumerable times. In August 2001, just three months after surgery, blood work revealed my system was rejecting the liver. During that stay at Johns Hopkins, I watched myself turn more and more yellow. I also developed pancreatitis, a severely painful condition. Images revealed to the doctors that there was scarring in a duct between the transplanted organ and the native opening which caused a remarkable stricture. They solved the problem by inserting a stent into the affected area via a procedure called an ERCP. Dr. Paul Thuluvath performed the initial stent placement, and then, every month for about five months, another ERCP and stent replacement. When I visited the outpatient center, month after month, I became intimately acquainted with the staff. Upon arrival, I was greeted, "Ah, Mrs. Spiese, how are you? So nice to see you again."

As you know by now, a transplant patient must take immunosuppressants to prevent rejection of the organ which is regarded by t-cells as a foreign body. Because of our compromised immune systems, transplant recipients are very susceptible to bacteria, colds, and other contaminating invasions. Although we often do not, we should avoid children, who carry lots of germs, working in the soil, and being around those who are coughing and sneezing.

I have been hospitalized with undiagnosed infections, Lyme disease, and atrial fibrillation. My resistance to germs of all sorts is very low. But through it all, I have kept a positive attitude and survived. To be functioning well one day and near death the next has made my life seem like a dream.

Often, throughout this walk, people have wondered why I am not embittered. The experience of living with uncertainty, I have finally realized, has been a wondrous gift. I have learned to seize the moment. Since even early on, Steve and I had such firsthand knowledge of life's fragility, our relationship leapt forward, so to speak, in maturity. The marriages of some of our college friends failed, perhaps because they did not know how to cherish one another and life itself.

Whispering "thanks" in my heart has become *the secret of life* for me. To worry, to complain, to think of the worst possible scenario is a waste of valuable energy. I am not recommending that you lie to yourself when trouble, illness, or injury comes. Rather, direct your energy into positive thought to reserve energy for healing, both physically and emotionally.

I have found the act of giving thanks for an experience, breathing through the pain, whether physical or emotional, and saying, "Thank you, more," a very valuable tool. Often, when I injured my leg with a bump or a fall from a bike, when I was low on potassium and the IV rapidly pumped the salt into my burning veins, Steve reminded me to shift my consciousness with these simple words, "Thank you. More."

Long before Oprah Winfrey advised her audience to keep a gratitude journal to help shift an attitude from negativity to thankfulness, I had made a practice of giving thanks for the little things: for my feet on the floor in the morning, for the aroma of coffee, the chill of winter, or the beauty of my husband's smile. This became my practice with each new day.

While we were classmates at Wheaton, Alice gifted me with a little poster imprinted with the words from Kahlil Gibran's *The Prophet:*

To wake at dawn with a winged heart and give
Thanks for another day of loving.

She will never know what an immense role this mantra has played in my survival.

I am inexpressibly grateful for what I am—a child of the Universe, guided by the Source of all, and blessed. Thanks to my organ donor, I can walk and breathe. I can sing and laugh and love.

And live this dream.

Summer 2002
Just prior to Right Knee Replacement

Forever Friend Alice 2003

A SYNOPSIS OF MY DREAM

I stand atop a mountain overlooking virgin forest broken occasionally into patchwork sections by grass-carpeted, wildflower-sprinkled meadows. The climb up the mountain has been grueling, thwarted by precarious footing and seemingly insurmountable boulders and obstacles, physical and emotional, of every sort. I've pulled and stumbled for thirty-five of my forty-nine years. Is it any wonder I've been discouraged now and then? Can I be blamed for considering just letting go and falling into another dimension?

But something has held me up so that, with a sigh of relief, I've reached the top.

Now, what I really expected was a time to rest, an end to the nearly endless journey. The wind whispers over my face and arms. The sun kisses my face warmly until a gray cloud saunters over its cheery smile.

I sit on the pebbly plateau, hugging my knees. I close my eyes and rest my head against my aching legs. The sweet fine dust swirls around me, comforting, lulling, like the blanket that tucked me in every night as a child. The day is ending, and soon, I will be in a dream world of my own imaginings. Ahhh, peace. Sweet release. The journey's done.

Then, suddenly, the cloud moves on. The sun beats down, glaring through eyelids closed, disturbing this sweet rest, urging me to look where its light falls now.

There is a whole new journey ahead. One that has its unknowns but that promises a brand-new landscape. The sun is still high in the sky. Evening will come, but not soon, not before I have tripped lightly down this mountainside, gently sloping, so different from the treacherous crag I climbed. Down and over untouched streams, unexplored forests, awakening the life within.

And like the life aroused in the forest, there rises a hope, a light of new life inside me. Each step will be a prized adventure, each breath a savored gift. Can there be a new me, energized to energize the worlds I touch?

As long as the light remains, I can take the trek. The forest beckons, its mystery calls. Do not be afraid. One step, then another. Even as I encounter newfound turf, I will yet always hold the wonders of the other side of the mountain.

But for now, I sit on the mountaintop. Perhaps I must spend a night or two or many, gaining strength, shedding the dead skin of hardworn and blistered hands and feet, ridding myself of habitual fears and suppressed anger. This time is as important as the climb up, as precious as the journey ahead.

Encounter the preying nighthawks, coexist with dark predators. Find courage and strength. Empty out the stale water and find cleansing for a fresh start, for an extraordinary day.

RESOURCES FOR THOSE WITH CHRONIC ILLNESS

www.thinkaboutyourlife.org
A site to set some of your own goals and to learn of other's hopes and fears and goals

https://www.gofundme.com/c/blog/financial-assistance-chronic-illness
Financial Assistance for Chronic Illness: Five Resources

https://medlineplus.gov/copingwithchronicillness.html
Treating depression, next steps, helping others who have chronic illness

Meditation and Spiritual Support:

Soulhub.com

https://chopracentermeditation.com/

https://mindworks.org/blog/meditation-for-healing/

CPSIA information can be obtained
at www.ICGtesting.com
Printed in the USA
BVHW081201090522
636525BV00020B/109